Praise for T

"People don't just buy what you sell, they buy what you stand for. They want to believe in your brand. The best way to convey that is through storytelling. **The Hook** takes the mystery out of the process and lets you peek behind the curtain of wonderful storytelling. How? By telling stories, of course. It is a masterfully written road map for how to use stories to connect on a deeper level with your customers. If you're not following his advice, you're missing out."

—Brent Niemuth, President & Chief Creative Officer, J.Schmid & Assoc. Inc.

"Here's the short story on **The Hook**: Go to school with Prof K. and learn to tell your brand story in a succinct, powerful, engaging way that matters to your customers. You'll be glad you did!"

—Andrea Syverson, Marketing Strategist, IER PARTNERS, INC.

"I wanted to begin this quote with a glib anecdote about how I took a relatively unknown brand of washing powder and within a few years, incorporating many of the marketing and storytelling techniques of Prof. Krevolin, I transformed that brand into the number one washing powder in the world with grosses in the billions! Instead, I will just say that his teachings contained in this book are an oasis from the same old reheated poppycock present in most marketing seminars and books. Instead of relying on lists of information, his book moves like a good story—in keeping with his emphasis on narrative and storytelling. Learn from him. Enjoy his lessons. Be inspired to tap into your natural brilliance and that of your colleagues!"

—Simon Clift, Former Chief Marketing Officer, Unilever

"Real leaders don't boss, they lead by inspiring and educating through great stories that engage consumers and are retained by them. Let master storyteller Prof. K. teach you how to tell business narratives that are transformative and re-energize your leadership!"

—Ritch K. Eich, Author and Former Chief of Public Affairs, Stanford University Medical Center

"The power of story is undeniable. In **The Hook**, Rich Krevolin clearly demonstrates why storytelling can move your audience and he gives you practical tools and techniques for crafting your own compelling narratives. If you're looking for ways to connect more deeply with your customers and your teams, the techniques in this book will help you do exactly that."

—Mike Figliuolo, Managing Director of *thought***LEADERS** and author of *One Piece of Paper* and *Lead Inside the Box*

"In this insightful, engaging, and highly entertaining book, Professor K. illuminates what are perhaps the most important elements of human experience—stories. Stories shape our beliefs and actions, they define us in context of other people. They are the truth as each of us perceives it. So-called 'rational' adults may want to relegate stories to children's play or entertainment; they do so at their peril, particularly in business. Krevolin demonstrates why story works and how to craft and tell them. Most importantly, he stresses the power of authenticity in stories and storytelling and illuminates a path to success in today's media where customers don't merely hear and buy into stories (or not), they are active participants in the process. *The Hook* is a master class in business that shows you how to build success exponentially with a tool every child knows—the power of a well-told story."

—Christopher Byrne, Marketing Consultant, Toy Expert and Author of *Funny Business*

"The best way to demonstrate the power of stories in business is, of course, to tell great stories. Richard Krevolin does exactly that in his latest book, **The Hook**. Business leaders can learn a lot from Hollywood screenwriters, and Krevolin's book serves as an important bridge between those two worlds."

—Victor Prince, Managing Director of DiscoveredLOGIC and Author of *Lead Inside the Box*

The
Hook

How to Share Your Brand's
Unique Story to Engage Customers,
Boost Sales, and Achieve
Heartfelt Success

FOREWORD BY HARRY BECKWITH
author of *Selling the Invisible*

Richard Krevolin

THE HOOK

EDITED BY ROGER SHEETY

TYPESET BY KRISTIN GOBLE

Cover design by Howard Grossman

Printed in the U.S.A.

To order this title, please call toll-free 1-800-CAREER-1 (NJ and Canada: 201-848-0310) to order using VISA or MasterCard, or for further information on books from Career Press.

The Career Press, Inc.

12 Parish Drive

Wayne, NJ 07470

www.careerpress.com

Library of Congress Cataloging-in-Publication Data

CIP Data Available Upon Request.

ACKNOWLEDGMENTS

This book would not have been possible without the help of hundreds of people who have contributed in both large and small ways to helping me complete a finished manuscript. So now, in advance, I'd like to apologize to anyone whose name I may have inadvertently forgotten and acknowledge below as many people as I possibly can remember:

A big thanks to Nancy Cohen, who urged me to write this book, and to my agent, Paula Munier, for garnering interest in this book, and to Renee, for her support through the process.

There were many great people who contributed interviews and/or forewords, so they should be mentioned: Shekar Khosla, Anila Shrivastava, Harry Beckwith, Terri Alpert, Trevor Garlick, Al Pirozzoli, Frank Myer, Joel Klettke, Kathy Copas, Michael Simon, Katja Bressette, Shalini Chandra, Abhijit Ghosh, and Suchitra Paranji.

As well, I'd like to mention Bill Ohlemeyer, David Steel, Coach Bob Orgovan, Colleen Sell, Ana Magno, Martin Weigel, Mark Knauer, and everybody else who in one way or another contributed to help make this a better book.

And last but not least, I would like to send out heaps of gratitude to every client who has ever hired me to help them tell their stories better. This book is dedicated to you.

CONTENTS

Part 3: Narrative Typologies / 135

Part 4: Real-World Applications / 179

FOREWORD

By Shekar Khosla

We are entering a new phase of storytelling with the rise of social media. In this phase, what individual people with a widening radius of trust and global connectedness say about your brand can become more important than what you say about your own brand.

In this new normal, transparency is mandated, and having an experienced and inspiring partner as you commercialize your brand promise is an asset. I found in Richard Krevolin just the kind of partner I was looking for while managing Unilever's Asia Pacific Skin business and building future corporate capabilities. He gave us a master class in story crafting and brand narratives. It was a powerful and essential workshop that showed me that good marketing is, in the end, really just good storytelling.

Ever since meeting Richard in that workshop many years ago, I have utilized many of his powerful strategies for leveraging the basic tenets of storytelling to build and sustain iconic brands. I have, indeed, come away richer after having been exposed to his teaching and I know you will do the same after reading this book.

In the end, his take on marketing and business is too valuable to be limited to only being accessible in his workshops, so I am grateful and happy that he has finally agreed to get it all down in a book. Finally, all this fascinating and useful information will now be accessible to the world. So then, you may ask, what exactly is contained in this volume?

Well, this book is a compelling exposition by Professor Krevolin on how storytelling is even more relevant in today's digitized world. Storytelling is widely recognized as our natural response to memory, with the stories we recall becoming a part of our identities. However, with the rise of social media, the challenge for iconic and local brands is that the brand stories are no longer only being crafted by brand custodians, but also by consumers.

Take your time reading this book by a master teacher. Entertaining, informative, and, of course, filled with heaps of wonderful stories, there's too much information contained herein to rush through it. Refer to it again and again through the course of your life as you continue to compose new brand narratives.

And as Prof. K. says, "Be bold. Be brave. Hook 'em by telling better stories."

—Shekar Khosla, Chief Marketing Officer,
Kellogg Asia Pacific and Africa

FURTHER FOREWORD

By Harry Beckwith

This is beyond doubt: You and I are story-based.

When humans first appeared on earth, we gathered around fires for warmth. And all teachers, leaders, and entertainers shared one trait in common, regardless of culture or country; they were the men and women who told the stories. Stories conveyed historic events, life lessons, diverse perspectives, and the chance to learn from mistakes and successes. They inspired emotion and action, and offered a sense of healing, community, and interconnection. Stories wove the original "World Wide Web" when they were shared by travelers to and from distant lands.

The great religions sprang from storytellers, too. Moses, Mohammed, and Jesus of Nazareth were gifted at the art. The great military leaders have been, too, not least of all because the world's hardest sell is to convince a young man or woman to risk his or her life for their country.

We crave stories, in part, because we were made this way. "The oldest neural pathway in the human brain," a renowned brain scientist once told me, "is for the narrative. Our brains—and from that, our entire beings—are hardwired for stories."

Look around you, everywhere. For example, what is our evening news? It's a series of stories, told one after the other. We are surrounded by stories. Our movies, novels, and plays? Stories. Our dances, artistic creations, favorite songs, or TV shows? Stories. The stuff of every issue of *People* (or any other magazine or newspaper), our everyday gossip to our friends, how we perceive ourselves and our relationships? All stories.

The skeptics and the bottom liners step in now and argue, "Business is different. Business is rational." They insist, "Business is selling a good product at a good price."

Well, no and no. Success in business is about offering something that appeals to you and me. And nothing appeals to you and me, and every other you and me, than a well-told story.

Richard Krevolin realized this and built a business teaching businesses the art he learned from making movies: the art of storytelling. These are his lessons, nicely conveyed, of course, and I urge you to learn them. They will make you a more effective leader, teacher, and marketer, too.

And they're a lot more fun to be with while just sitting around a fire.

—Harry Beckwith, Business Advisor and
Author of Amazon's #2 Rated
Business Book of All Time, *Selling the Invisible*

Part 1: Why Stories?

CHAPTER 1

A New Story Vision

The bait has to taste good to the fish, not the fisherman.
—Anonymous

How do innovative leaders and companies hook their target markets? How do they educate, inspire, and sell their products, services, and overall brand? They craft resonant, emotionally moving stories that ignite real and positive transformation both inside and outside their companies.

Wait!

They do this by telling stories? C'mon, really? Stories? Aren't they just something you read to kids to put them to sleep? And how do narratives relate to everything they teach in "B" school about cost-effectivity metrics and...

Yes, yes, yes, you can get an MBA and employ all the best metrics in the world, but if you can't create an emotional connection with your target audience/market, then nothing else really matters, does it?

And how do you connect and engage with other human beings? Well, there's really only one way that's been proven to work with human beings over the past million years. You hook 'em with a story. Yep, you craft and share narratives!

Narratives in the digital age

In an always-on consumer world, the role of marketing needs to change from a batch process of sequential campaigns into a trading room monitoring and engaging with the ebb and flow of conversations happening in a digital space and context. It is, therefore, not just about storytelling anymore (which is a self-contained unit of beginning, middle, and end that has already occurred), but about timeless, ever-evolving brand narratives that you must create and control.

Marketing used to be about creating a myth and selling it. Now it is about finding a truth and sharing it. We are moving beyond traditional one-way, top-down storytelling to multi-level, interactive brand narratives. So what exactly are brand narratives?

Brand narratives must emerge from answering "Why does a brand exist?" and not from "What does it sell?" or "How does it sell?" Brand narratives are about you; they are created by you and consumers in an effort to find meaning. Brand narratives are the core of a long-term conversation with continuous engagement that always points back to the brand purpose.

These days, for brands to truly be successful, they must do more than just provide information about their qualities. They must also tell a story. And that story must align with consumer needs. In this book, I will look at how smart brands can go out into the world and create meaning for customers and consumers via the construction of brand narratives.

You will also learn about the psychological underpinnings of why a story really does persuade and influence. Exploring the latest discoveries in scientific research on brain chemistry and psychology, I will trace how we, as human beings, physiologically respond to and are moved by story. You will then learn exactly what is and isn't a "good story well told" and in doing so, you will learn how to use human responses to story to ally your company with your target audience and generate more sales.

I will emphasize this again and again in this book: *A core concept about brand narratives is the understanding that your brand or product must not be the hero of the story you are telling. Instead, your brand or product must be the helpful ally that allows the consumer to reach their goals, to achieve their potential, to become the person that they were meant to be and couldn't be without your product.*

Capeche, paisan?

Then, I will define the purpose of your brand—its own DNA—and how to translate that into a narrative form that will remain vital and engaging far beyond any label, Website, or promotional video. Understanding all aspects of your company's unique story is crucial to your ongoing and future success, both within and outside of your organization.

In the ensuing pages, I will also discuss relevant aspects of how stories fit into business systems (for example, your brand proposition, your packaging, your product sensory feel, etc.) and offer examples of real world applications across multiple industries (such as banking, consumer products, durables, luxury, mass products) and across the globe.

In this age of social media and digital storytelling, if you understand storytelling, you can dictate and manage the content architecture for your brand and, in doing so, also work to shape the story told by your customers and digital consumers. Brand narratives have the power to emotionally differentiate any brand from all of the others in the same category. I will further explore how, with the rise of social media, storytelling has now moved toward brand narratives told by many creators and constantly revised by consumers in different forms of digital communication and social media.

Finally, I will share a specific process of brand narrative construction that you can begin using immediately for more effective marketing, and I will provide real-world examples of successful narrative-driven work that has increased engagement and sales.

The rise and fall and rise of storytelling

In an age where people feel more busy and harried than ever, yet are bombarded by more advertising/media choices and product options than ever, how do you convey your company's message and ensure that it gets seen, heard, and absorbed in the way you desire?

Now, more than ever, great storytelling is necessary. However, a series of questions inevitably arise:

> Has the art of storytelling been extinguished by the blinding white-hot glow of computer monitor screens and PowerPoint slides?
> If story has been supplanted by technology, can it ever be resurrected?
> And even if it can, why should we bother trying?
> How do you find your own unique way and voice amidst the myriad storytellers out there?
> Why storytelling and why now in the context of a business?

These are all valid questions. And all can be answered with this simple refrain:

The secret to successful communication, persuasion, and engagement lies in good storytelling, and this book will provide a simple, well-researched, and proven methodology to do so.

For any businessperson who cares about these things, it is imperative that they attempt to reacquaint themselves with the art of storytelling in order to ensure future success and engagement with customers and consumers.

And so I have written this book as a stop-gap—a primer on an art form that is being discussed increasingly, but one that is also disappearing and seeming ever more elusive. It is intended to serve as a sort of defibrillator paddle, if you will, to revive and inspire new life in the practice of storytelling today. It is a guidebook, a beacon of light to illustrate how you might utilize stories to enhance the success of your business, both inside and outside your brick and mortar walls.

Though I will introduce you to a sampling of helpful narrative rules and methodologies, it is key to remember that the essence of good storytelling is that your narratives must be nuanced and original, not rigid and formulaic. This gives you a competitive edge right from the start. All the rules are merely guard rails on the two-way story highway in which you will soon be speeding down on your journey into the world of creating and sharing brand narratives.

Remember: You are the one who can tell the story of your business best. You just need to be open to the fact that narratives are not born overnight nor created easily. Even the best storytellers craft and refine their stories over and over again in order to get them right. But it is you, and no other, who knows exactly whom your story needs to speak to. In this understanding of your audience lies the key to constructing the right stories well. And, hence, therein lies your power.

Let me add a little side note: Such a journey will certainly be more rousing and entertaining than a white paper, an accounting spreadsheet, or a heavy, bullet-pointed PowerPoint presentation.

"Hold on! Forget it," you say. "I'm not a natural storyteller. There is no way I will ever be able to do this."

And I say, "Nonsense! You can do this and soon you will be creating fresh and powerful brand narratives."

Being a bit hesitant here is natural. In fact, in almost every storytelling seminar I have taught during the last 25 years, three types of questions and concerns always seem to arise:

1. Question: Is storytelling a natural talent, a God-given gift that can't be taught?

    Answer: No. Anyone can learn to do it effectively. I've seen it happen repeatedly, regardless of the nationality of the storyteller or their comfort level in front of an audience.

2. Question: Are there guidelines or proven methodologies that might help in the construction of a good story if someone is not a natural storyteller?

    Answer: Absolutely! And I will share several of them through the course of the book so you can immediately begin telling more compelling, life-changing stories. After having led classes and workshops around the world and having written books, screenplays, stage plays, comic book scripts, speeches, commercial/advertising scripts, and even worked on opening statements and closing arguments for courtroom cases, I've noticed a series of rules that come into play every time with each individual project. Yes, there are specific unifying guidelines that can be implemented during the act and art of storytelling. When you understand the DNA of your brand, you can then craft an appropriate story to emotionally convey the necessary information in a way that will engage your target audience.

3. Question: Stories are all well and good to be used sparingly, but in the end, aren't statistics, metrics, lists, and bullet points the most powerful and effective way to market?

Answer: This is a good question, and I think the answer is simply that statistics and bullet points feel safe, especially when a lot of money is at stake. So relying on statistics instead of stories feels less risky. And, unlike statistical analysis, storytelling isn't an exact science. As a result, there's an inherent uncertainty associated with storytelling. Tell the wrong story and it can hurt you. So care needs to be taken. Yet, tell the right story, and the benefits can be far greater than the result of any statistical analysis.

Steve Jobs used great design backed by great storytelling that bucked trends in statistical analysis. He knew that if he could tell the right story about his products, he could create fanatical consumers, and he didn't need metrics to prove to himself this was correct.

A modest proposal

So here's my modest proposal: Instead of thinking of storytelling as a scary prospect, or this system as a straitjacket that will confine you, try to think of it as a wide highway that will take you where you want to go, give you free berth to go there at your own pace, and allow you to employ your own style along the way.

Maybe the best way to think of these guidelines is in terms of a metaphor. I believe the rules of storytelling are quite similar to those of a sonnet. You see, with a sonnet, at first there seems to be very little flexibility. The rhyme sequence is pre-established. There can only be 14 lines. It must be written in iambic pentameter.

But even with these constraints, stop for a moment and think of how many gorgeous and different sonnets have been written through the years. Open your mind to the freedom that exists within these defined parameters once these parameters are understood and embraced.

The new agenda for narratives

We live in a new era in which corporations can no longer just worship the bottom line of profits. Consumers and customers increasingly want to purchase and be associated with brands that practice business with responsibility and social consciousness.

Fortunately, most companies today have both a compelling story to tell and an array of innovative, game-changing products and services that are the epitome of this new emphasis on social responsibility.

But how do you get people excited about inanimate objects? How do you create the necessary awareness of your new products and services?

You do it by telling your story well.

Every company today needs to craft both personal signature stories for the founders, leaders, and employees of the company, as well as brand narratives that represent the essence of your brand to the world. In doing so, you can engage consumers in such a memorable and emotionally positive way that you then become their go-to brand.

In a nutshell, if you tell us moving, credible, and compelling stories, we will like you, we will care about you, and, as a result, we will want to buy from you. Every good salesperson knows this. And so, by the very act of buying this book and thinking differently about stories, you are well on your way to gaining a new *story vision* that will hook your target audience.

If your signature brand narrative is told well and truly embodies the DNA of your company, you will have a tool that helps sales and also furthers the meaning and purpose of your brand both in internal and external corporate communications.

The road to igniting transformation

You must dare to share your unique story with the world! If you transform how you transmit information about your business, you can become more effective at conveying your message and garnering the response you desire. Instead of simply offering lists, bullet points, or statistics, your job is to create innovative brand narratives that convey what you do in a more compelling, engaging, and emotionally resonant way—whether these stories are your own personal signature stories or narratives about your people, products, or services.

Through the course of this book, I will share with you tons of tips, parameters, and guidelines relating to storytelling. I will give you a good sense of how storytelling works and some of the rules that govern this realm. One small note of caution: Possible side effects of story creation can include more fun and enjoyment, inspiration, a greater sense of community, and the enhanced success of your company.

So now the ancient journey begins anew. I invite you to join me in venturing forth and taking chances within the circumscribed, but still wide, territorial berth of good storytelling.

CHAPTER 2

Prof. K.'s Personal Brand Narrative

|||||||||||||||||||||||||||||||||||||||||||||||||||||||||||||||||||||||||||||||||||||||||||||||||||||||||||||||||||||||||||||||||||||||||||||||||||||

Memory is not a neutral act. Memory is an act of construction.
We don't remember all the facts; we remember a group of facts
that are tied together in a story that makes sense of our reality.
—Rabbi Irwin Kula, as quoted in
Making Light in Terezin

As this book is about storytelling, it wouldn't be right if I went any further without sharing a personal story with you.

Once upon a time, there was a Hollywood screenwriter, storyteller, and script doctor (me) who started to notice that the principles that applied to fixing a story for the silver screen also applied to fixing a story for a CEO's speech, a TV commercial, a business plan, a manager's PowerPoint presentation, and a salesperson's pitch. It is a story about how it became abundantly clear to me through the years that the principles of storytelling, regardless of the endless diversity of stories, are universal and unchanging. It is a story about how I started teaching these precepts to businesspeople who, at first, did not think of themselves as creative, but soon showed great aptitude for adapting and applying these principles and quickly became masterful story-sellers.

Yet, I know there are skeptics out there. The "Yeah, butters" who find different approaches suspect and always seem to be saying:

"Yeah, but can this stuff really be taught?"

"Yeah, but can you really compel anyone to buy anything no matter how good your story is?!"

"Yeah, but what about...?"

Simply put, I think these questions and comments are connected and all revolve around the issue of communication. Whether you want to write a story to sell a bar of soap or you want to write a screenplay to sell to Hollywood, it's all the same. It all comes down to the story you create.

Good storytelling is always effective. Storytelling works. Think about it. When a bunch of people are all vying for the same position, who gets the job? The person who tells the best story about himself or herself does.

When a company is in trouble, what kind of CEO is able to lead the company out of the red and keep his or her job? Why, of course, it's the CEO who can truly communicate an inspiring vision for the future of their company.

What about the best salespeople you've ever met? What common trait did they share besides good hair and nice shoes? Storytelling skills! Inherent in being a good salesperson is being a good storyteller.

Yes, I admit it. I see the world through a story lens and through narrative-colored glasses. So, now, I think it's time for me to stand up and publicly state, "Hi. My name is Richard and I am a story addict."

Yes, I spend eight hours or more a day writing my own stories, consulting with people on their stories, and writing books about telling stories. In more than 25 years of learning about and sharing stories, I have come to know—and can help you to determine—story structure, character development, creating a world, and when a story is (or is not) working. And if it is broken, I can help you fix it.

I make no pretenses of knowing a great deal about many different things, especially in the business world. But I do have many years of expertise in one specific field: *storytelling!*

I know how to tell a good story and how to teach others to tell a good story. I have spent nearly three decades writing stories, studying storytelling, and teaching about the telling of stories. This book is the culmination of those three decades of work. It is an effort to articulate all that I have learned about storytelling in a clear and accessible manner. And, in keeping with my storytelling theme, much of it will be delivered through anecdotes and narratives.

When you tell a story well, you can make people laugh or cry. You can make them feel good about you, a product, a service, or a concept you are offering. When you tell a story really well, you can get people so excited that they will pay good money to hear that story again or to be part of it by purchasing the product or service being offered.

Remember that the power of storytelling does not apply to only so-called "creative" professions. The lawyer who tells the best story in court is the one who gains the confidence of the jury. The real estate agent who tells the best story about the house she has just put on the market is the one who gets the sale. The public relations professional who tells the most interesting story is the one who gets the press coverage for his client. The teacher who tells the best stories about the subject is always the one whose students are the most attentive and successful.

In essence, we are born to communicate with each other through stories and programmed as human beings to directly process information via stories.

Prof. K.'s personal narrative

So let me backtrack for a second and tell my story. During the past 25 years, I have been fortunate to make a living creating narratives across different genres: fiction and nonfiction, stage plays, and screenplays. In addition, I have been a professor of dramatic writing in the undergraduate and graduate classrooms of USC Cinema School, UCLA Film School, Emerson College, and Ithaca College.

From there, I started lecturing extensively to aspiring storytellers at writer's conferences and film festivals around the country. Then, many writers who heard my lectures started hiring me to privately consult with them on their stories. For many years, this was my focus. I wrote, taught, and coached writers. My work with storytellers was essentially limited to the world of Hollywood production companies, wanna-be Hollywood screenwriters, and a few playwrights and novelists.

Several years ago, I was asked to be one of the featured speakers at a conference on storytelling. There was no pay for the presenters and I would have to cover all travel, meal, and hotel expenses through the weekend. However, the conference was one I thought would be well worth the time and expense. I believed it would enable me to share my skills and "tricks of the trade" with a specific audience that was seeking help with manifesting their aspirations. At the same time, I thought it would help build my storytelling lecturing business by reaching those in the industry who wanted to hire experienced teachers of the craft. So I agreed to participate.

Only 12 people showed up for my lecture in a room that seated 200. Though I gave it my all and my talk went well, it was admittedly a bit deflating. Despite being excited to present and grateful for the positive response from those who did attend, I must confess I felt an initial sense of disappointment in sharing my passion with only 12 people, none of whom approached me that day about my story-consulting services.

I drove back to L.A. and tried to forget about it. Then, a few days later, I got a call from one of the other speakers, one of the leading storytelling experts in Hollywood. She said she'd recently gotten a call from a major global brand that wanted to fly her to an exotic foreign country to teach a week-long seminar on storytelling. Though she wished she could go, she already had a booking that week. She told me she had been one of the 12 attendees at my lecture during the previous weekend and that she'd recommended me for the job. She wanted to know whether I was interested in talking to them.

Was I interested? Yes!

Her recommendation led to my getting not only that job but a whole series of jobs with that company, as well as with other companies. In fact, it jump-started a whole new path in my career—helping businesses and entrepreneurs to achieve and sustain greater success with storytelling. And it was all because I presented at that one conference, which I'd originally thought had not been worth my time.

The lesson to me was abundantly clear: We are always writing our own stories in our head, and the story I had been writing in mine was short-sighted. I had come to believe that because I had spent a good deal of time and money on the conference and hadn't gotten any immediate consulting jobs from it, it wasn't worthwhile. Well, that story turned out to be erroneous!

Often in life, we don't know what will come from our efforts. Even though there were only 12 people in the audience, I still gave 110 percent in my lecture. As it turned out, one of those 12 people was impressed enough that she recommended me for a job, which ended up changing the course of my life.

So I rewrote my story in my head and learned a good lesson. When you're doing your job, you never know how your efforts might have a positive impact on others and, in turn, on your own life. In other words, when you interact with others, there is always a chance that the person you are sitting next to in a workshop, on a plane, or in a restaurant, for example, could be instrumental in furthering you along an exciting new path in your life.

My story, part two: the sequel

My story doesn't just end there. After all, I had a job to do working with a team of global brand managers for a huge multinational hair care brand and a group of ad executives at J. Walter Thompson (JWT). They were all seasoned professionals in a realm that was new to me. So, before we first spoke, I was nervous. How could I really help them? Yet, at the same time, I must admit that I was also quite intrigued by the challenge. I set up a date and time for a phone conference to discuss things further.

In my initial phone conversation with the global brand director and the JWT worldwide director in charge of hair care, they both asked me only one thing: "As a Hollywood story expert, do you believe it's possible to tell real stories, compelling hair dramas—you know, stories about the real hair problems that real women face on a daily basis—in less than 30 seconds? Can it be done? Will it work?"

I answered, "Absolutely! As long as you're willing to follow the basic precepts of good storytelling."

"Okay then, fine," one of them said. "But remember. In a 30-second commercial, once you include our product shot and product demo, you really only have 22 seconds left."

"No problem." I replied. "A story is a story, whether it runs the two-hour length of a feature film or only 22 seconds. It's just that the less time you have to tell the story, the more adept you must be at establishing your characters, the conflict, and the three-act structure."

As if in a Hollywood movie, the next thing I knew, I was in a fancy hotel in Havana, Cuba, of all places, lecturing in a large room filled with both brand and ad execs from all over the world. I was articulating the principles of story to them, and we began to create a classic structure that would work for 22-second hair dramas. But, alas, we hit a bump.

As happens in all dramatically interesting stories (more on this later), conflict and tension arose. I began getting a heck of a lot of opposition from some of the executives. This story thing was new and different and, well, a bit uncomfortable for many of them. And they were resisting it!

You see, 80 to 90 percent of all commercials are not story-based; they are premise-based. In other words, there is a much greater comfort level with TV spots that convey specific product benefits to the consumer and that do not tell stories.

The executives asked for an example of a modern, premise-based TV commercial. So I screened an award-winning commercial for Tabasco sauce set in the Louisiana backwoods. The thrust of the commercial is based upon what the good people at Tabasco want you to know: Their product is *hot!*

They dramatize this product benefit by showing you a hot afternoon on the bayou. A mosquito sucks the blood of a Cajun guy who has just ingested a meal covered with Tabasco sauce. The mosquito then flies away. A moment later, the hot, Tabasco-sauce-filled blood overpowers the mosquito and he explodes. *Bam!* (You can find this commercial and others like it at YouTube.com.)

It's a funny spot. (I was not involved in making it; I was just a fan.) More importantly to the people at Tabasco, it is a good dramatization of what they need you to understand about their product: Their sauce really is *hot, hot, hot!*

But is it a story? No. And, if it were rewritten into a story, could it be an even better commercial? I think so. Let me explain further. In this spot, the main character is the Cajun guy who is hanging out. If we rewrote the spot so that at the beginning we see that he is plagued by mosquitoes biting him and terrorizing him all day and night, we would feel for him and understand his dilemma. Then, when he fails to defeat the mosquitoes with conventional means and decides to use Tabasco sauce instead, we would cheer for him when he achieves victory. This, then, is an example of taking a good spot and adding story elements to make it great.

The JWT executives heard my argument and got it. They soon came to see that what they were resisting and had seen as a potential problem was really an opportunity. Because so many of the commercials around the globe are not story-based, there is a huge opening here for something different and more impactful: good storytelling.

The previously mentioned global brand director saw this opening and that is why he had brought us together. He believed in the power of story and he urged us to capitalize on it. So we did. Led by his vision and the backing of a courageous, pioneering ad agency, we forged ahead to get to the heart of some hair stories.

Together, we worked to create a new kind of commercial storytelling that fit the world of hair care: real stories based upon real women with real hair problems. We vowed to develop 22-second hair dramas that could do more than just demonstrate the qualities of a new shampoo and would also, through story, convey brand characteristics, product insights, and specific personality traits and sensibilities.

Our goal was clear and simple. By telling a good story about this brand of shampoo, we would ensure that when consumers walked by and saw it on the supermarket shelf next to several other brands, they would have a positive emotional response to it, caused by the commercial stories they had seen and enjoyed.

As a result, they would prefer this brand, choosing it over others. In other words, our hair dramas fostered a feeling of kinship toward the brand, an emotional closeness, creating a loyalty to this brand. Every marketer's dream come true, right?

The success of our intentionally adding storytelling to the ad campaign was confirmed, yet again, in a recent conversation I had with an executive who no longer works with the brand but did years ago. She said there was a huge spike in sales when we did the hair dramas. Then, when a new team was brought in and they went back to the old-school mode of showing models flipping their hair and animation of molecules onscreen, sales plummeted and the brand never really recovered.

Storytelling, if done right, can help captivate and capture the brand's target market. But the key thing here is that the storytelling must be done right. You must clearly establish the insights and themes you want your stories to convey, and then you must execute them perfectly to effectively communicate that information. In doing so, you can differentiate your product from all the rest and really story-sell.

I must admit, though, that during this time another bump in the road kept reappearing over and over again. Many "creative" execs at the agency did not like the idea of being bound by the rules of storytelling. They tried to reject what they thought of as a straitjacket that limited their infinite creativity.

I refused to accept this. Rules are not a negative thing. As this book will make abundantly clear, you do not have to break any rules to be creative. There is tremendous room inside the box; there are millions of sonnets out there. And the rules aren't straitjackets; they're merely inspirational guidelines!

Speaking of rules, many of the basic tenets of dramatic structure came into being for only one reason: They work! They were first outlined by Aristotle more than 2,000 years ago, and they have not changed much since then because our underlying human nature hasn't changed much since then. Aristotle stated that drama functions in the following three act structure:

Act 1: Set up/inciting incident/dilemma.

Act 2: Develop story further/crisis/decision and action.

Act 3: Climax/resolution.

Just look at every hit TV show and blockbuster Hollywood film and you will see that they all follow certain basic story parameters and precepts. Yet, even though these stories follow these certain circumscribed parameters, they are each very different.

Rules can be liberating if they are understood and not seen as confining. They give you structure. And they allow you tremendous freedom within this structure.

So, in each group that I worked with, we resolved to follow the rules but also try to stretch them a bit. I was impressed with the corporate culture of the companies I worked with. Female and male executives and entire sales teams yearned to put their own personal stamp on the creation of spots that told real and unique stories, rather than simply having every single one featuring slow-motion shots of gorgeous women flipping their gorgeous heads of hair. It's easy to go online and find many bad examples of hair flip commercials, as well as a bevy of spots that make fun of such ridiculousness.

JWT copywriters from around the world generated a series of new hair dramas. Stories—moving, powerful, emotional stories—were told in 22 seconds or less. I'm thrilled to report that one of the first hair drama spots we worked on together, entitled "Lecture Hall," was voted by Chinese viewers as one of their 10 "Most Admired Commercials" for that year. And it was the only personal-care brand to make the list, along with brands like VW, Pepsi, and Intel. The success of the campaign was a real tribute to all the people, both marketing and advertising agency execs, who worked so hard to do something different.

At this point you may be wondering, "Well, that's great if you are a big corporation that can afford to hire a creative agency like J. Walter Thompson, but what if you are a small business with only a minimal marketing budget?"

Well, for starters, the secrets of storytelling are accessible to anyone who has an open mind, a willingness to look at your story from different perspectives and then rework it, and a desire to learn and grow.

Think about it. If, through storytelling, you can integrate your product's brand benefits into your audience's larger life purpose, then haven't you created a deep connection that can really pay off?

Do you, as a marketer, have the bravery to subsume your brand into your story? Do you have the courage to write a new story that incorporates the product benefit in the context of your consumer's life? And if you can pull this off, don't you think many of your customers will want to have a long-term relationship with you?

In summary

There are universal rules behind good storytelling, but now with the rise of new media forms and social media, the way you need to tell stories has changed. We used to focus on product benefits. But today, in a world where consumers are inundated with choices, if you want your products and services to be noticed and adopted, you must go beyond functionality and be rooted in a purpose that engages people.

A product or service must go beyond a transaction or list of functions. You need to provide an experience that adds value to someone's life through fulfilling a need or satisfying a desire. You need to connect with your customers via a strong brand narrative that translates into all forms of social media.

Every touch point that a consumer has with you and your product must revolve around your Brand DNA and the narrative that emerges from it.

I created this book so that I can share my more than 25 years of knowledge of storytelling with you and that we might co-create a new brand narrative for you that will spark discussion, engage emotions, and foster loyalty.

Brand narratives are more than just a group of facts about you. They must place these facts in an emotional context that engages consumers. And narratives are the world's oldest and most effective way to do this.

Together, let's explore the stories being told in the business world today. The age of the one-way narrative street is over. We are seeing stories as the basis of a conversation in which you have a chance to frame the narrative and set the tone for the conversation in which stories are shared by all: brand creators, marketers, users, and customers.

True, you cannot dictate the conversation and, thus, control your consumer's stories. But if you understand the need for story and why it conveys the Brand DNA of your company, that story will become the touchstone for all conversation about your company or product. And there are rules as to why stories work and what you can do to improve their emotional impact.

So rewrite and activate your brand by learning about the story you are telling and how you can improve that story so that it will both frame the conversation about your product and company, as well as inspire consumer stories that build off your narrative.

Don't let the conversations on social media overtake you and alter the way the world sees you and your product. Instead, dictate the rules of the conversation and create the discussion.

After reading this book, you will be able to use your new game-changing knowledge of storytelling to set the tone for offline and online narratives that will lead to the future success of your company and product.

And always, "Be bold. Be brave. Hook 'em by telling better stories."

CHAPTER 3

Humans and Storytelling

You are not welcome until customers like you. And
they won't like you until they listen to you. And
they won't listen to you if you open your pitch with
bulleted copy points of your product's superiority.
—Luke Sullivan, *Hey Whipple, Squeeze This*

Like most people, I've loved stories since I was a young child. I
remember looking forward to weekends when I could hide in
the basement and read comic books and fantasy novels for hours
upon hours and escape into the world of great storytellers.

However, it was only when I was working on my MFA in screenwriting that I really started to think deeply about the construction
of narratives and their roles in our lives. This analytical study has
tarnished a bit of the glossy shine off of stories, but it has also given
me a much more profound appreciation for the power of engaging
narratives. So now, let us dive into the world of storytelling and

start to think more about the meaning and role that narratives play in all aspects of our daily lives.

The List Tribe vs. the Story Tribe

In purely Darwinian, evolutionary terms, what purpose might there be in human beings being more receptive to stories than to a list of facts?

Well, let's look back at the history of human beings and try to postulate an answer. What if, originally, there were two different types of tribes? Let's call one the Story Tribe and the other the List Tribe.

Tony, the leader of the List Tribe, turned to his people and said, "Yo, peeps, here is a list of things to do when you see a lion." He went on to articulate the 10 important things to do on his list.

At the same time, a few miles away in the jungle, Phil, the Story Tribe's leader, said, "Hey, dudes, did I ever tell you the story about how I evaded a lion when I was young?" He went on to tell his story while all the tribe members listened with rapt attention.

Then, members of both tribes went out into the jungle. Eventually, each group bumped into a lion. When this happened, people of the Story Tribe instantly remembered the story of how their leader evaded the lion, and they mimicked his actions and survived their encounter.

On the other hand, when members of the List Tribe confronted a lion, they stopped and thought, "Hmm, what exactly were the 10 important things I am supposed to do now and what was the order again?" And as they attempted to recall their list, they were eaten and removed from the gene pool. As a result, the List Tribe soon disappeared, and today I think it's fair to say that we are all the genetic offspring of the Story Tribe.

If we are all descendants of the Story Tribe and not the List Tribe, what does this mean for effective communication among fellow Story Tribe members?

Benjamin Franklin once said, "Tell me and I'll forget. Show me and I might remember. Involve me and I'll understand." And that's what a good Story Tribe member must do. You must tell a story that involves your intended audience.

If we agree with the assertion that stories are how we, as human beings, encode information that involves us and is memorable, then won't the right story be the key to your audience appreciating, understanding, retaining, and acting upon your message?

Let me give you an example. I have done some work with the great company Panera Bread. They are always introducing delicious new seasonal sandwiches and salads. It would be easy to just list the new combination of ingredients on the menu, but they know that's not enough. They are constantly telling stories about these ingredients and how they came to be part of Panera's current menu. The company has even been known to offer a story section on their Website with the description: "From kitchen and cooking tips to the inspiration behind our food, these are our stories of care and craft" (*www.panerabread.com/en-us/craftsmanship /stories.html*).

A well-engineered story can transform an audience's outlook, how they see you and your company, and their future choices about expenditures of money and time. Yes, of course, I know this sounds idealistic, but it's also true. We define our reality in terms of stories, and then we act on them. We naturally communicate and share ideas and information via stories. This is what makes them so effective. As a result, stories are the single best inspirational, motivational, and instructional tool that we have. Period.

For example, when the probiotic drink GT's Kombucha first came out, very few people had heard of Kombucha, an ancient Chinese drink made from fermented green tea. So each bottle featured a story of the origin of the drink; not how it was invented in China, but how GT, the owner of the company, started making Kombucha for his mother when she was battling cancer. When she beat the cancer, he decided to bottle it for a living. Sure, he lists the ingredients on the bottle, but it was his story that really got me interested in trying it. And now, along with many other Americans, I am hooked on it.

Here's an interesting legal side note. I do not know the specifics of what happened, but recently, the GT story featured on the label has changed. It now says, "GT Dave began bottling Kombucha in 1995 from his mother's kitchen." It no longer mentions his mother's battle with cancer. My best guess is that the wording of the original story was indirectly communicating that using this product can help one overcome cancer and could be construed as a legally suspect claim. So the story has changed to protect the brand, both in terms of legal issues and the brand equity. This, then, is a good lesson on the power of story and, at the same time, about how mistakes in a narrative's construction can be potentially harmful if not fully considered in advance.

As human beings, we are physiologically programmed to tell and receive stories, and genetically programmed to learn through them. Before there was PowerPoint, before there were books or even any form of written language, how did people learn? They told stories.

We know of pictograms and cave drawings, but it appears that the mass of information was passed down through an oral tradition of storytelling. The repository of the wisdom of the culture was entrusted to the tribal storyteller. Even in cultures without a tribal storyteller, around the campfire, or the hearth, or on the hunt, elders told stories to youngsters in order to inform, educate, and entertain. Those who listened and learned from these stories survived and passed down through the generations a genetic predisposition to assimilate and remember stories.

Thus, the human species evolved as story-beings. Call us *homo narrativus*.

C'mon, let's get irrational

Why stories? Why do they work? What do they do that lists don't?

Well, in a nutshell, they speak to the non-rational, the unconscious, and the emotional side of us all. This is hugely significant because it is clear that we are much more driven by irrational impulses than we would like to think. When Daniel Goleman talks about what he calls "primal leadership," he is speaking of this exact thing. Goleman states, "Great leaders move us. They ignite our passion and inspire the best in us. When we try to explain why they are so effective, we speak of strategy, vision, or powerful ideas. But the reality is much more primal: Great leadership works through the emotions" (*www.danielgoleman.info/topics/leadership/*).

And stories are a great way to access the emotions.

Sure, we pride ourselves on how smart, rational, and intelligent we are. We believe that the decisions we make are well-reasoned, logical conclusions resulting from the judicious weighing of facts. We believe that our memory is accurate, that we can look dispassionately at any and all subjects without bias and always reach an objective, well-thought-out decision.

Of course, this is completely false! *It's all wrong!* Advances in science and research today have shown that so much of what we think and do has nothing to do with rational, logical, conscious thought. Decision-making is not so simple after all.

Studies of people with damage to the part of their brains that deal with emotions show that they are essentially incapable of making well-thought-out decisions and, in essence, are incapable of functioning and living ordinary lives. Instead of being more rational and better decision-makers, they spend hours trying to make simple decisions that you and I make in a matter of seconds.

As one of my heroes, copywriting legend Bill Bernbach, said, "You can say the right thing about a product and nobody will listen. You've got to say it in such a way that people will feel it in their gut. Because if they don't feel it, nothing will happen" (*www .brainyquote.com/quotes/authors/w/william_bernbach.html*).

This point is well-illustrated in the excellent article "Deeply Understanding the Mind to Unmask the Inner Human," by Katja E. Bressette, director of strategic initiatives at Olson Zaltman Associates. In this thoughtful article, Bressette uses stories and examples to demonstrate her point. In fact, she cites five interrelated insights about how the mind works. These insights, drawn from current advances in several behavioral science disciplines, are:

- "95 percent of human thinking and emotion happens in the unconscious."
- "Humans think in neural activations (neural images), not words."
- "Metaphoric thinking is the basic mental process."
- "Stories are an integral part of making sense of the world, learning, and expressing ourselves."
- "Emotion is critical to how humans think, behave, and interpret the world."

I can hear the naysayers chiming in and saying, "Wait a second there, buddy. This is a list, not a story."

Okay, yes, there are stories in her article, but in this case Bressette chose to convey the core learnings of her article with a list, and I have chosen to share her list with you. I think this is a good example of when a list is the appropriate choice over a story. Bressette is writing a scholarly article, not creating a sell piece for a consumer product. For her particular audience, this is the right choice. With that said, it must be noted that this list is unlikely to be easily retained by any reader.

In the end, whether a person chooses to convey information via a list or a story, it must be conceded that many aspects of our lives are affected by our subconscious.

Let me give you an example. How often have you been driving and talking on the phone (with a wireless headset, I hope) only to realize that you've gone 20 miles and haven't thought about driving once the whole time? During that period, it's really your subconscious that's doing the driving. A series of autonomic actions have turned the car and pushed the brakes and kept you on the road without getting into an accident. All the while, your conscious mind was engaged in your phone conversation, not driving.

In many other aspects of life, as well, it is the subconscious that drives so many of our actions and choices. Why is this significant? Well, it's through metaphors and stories that we are able to tap into the subconscious, into what some call the "reptilian" part of the brain where emotions rule.

In *Talk Like TED*, Carmine Gallo analyzed hundreds of TED talks. He discovered that after seeing all these presentations, the most successful ones were "65 percent pathos, 25 percent logos, and 10 percent ethos." So yes, you need information, facts, and values. But the majority of what really sells and drives retention—the driving force behind your sales pitch—must be emotionally driven so that it appeals to the irrational. It's about pathos.

Driven to story

Another wonderful book, *Driven*, explores human nature and human drives. Written by Harvard Business School professors Paul R. Lawrence and Nitin Nohria, the book says, "Stories are basic to human memory process. The mind establishes a story line, with the memory of one event triggering the memory of the next. Early humans passed on knowledge primarily through the art of storytelling."

Nohria and Lawrence are studying human drives in terms of their marketing repercussions. But what they learned also applies to what you will do as a storyteller, because the more deeply you understand human drives, the better a storyteller you will be. If you truly understand human nature, you will also better understand the motives of your staff, clients, potential customers, and even the characters in your story.

Be a POSR

Human beings are not a *tabula rasa*, a clean slate. If you don't believe me, have a few kids and then get back to me. When you see several children from different gene pools and social backgrounds all pull back in terror when they see a snake or hear a lion roar, it becomes clear that we all have some responses that are innate and not conditioned.

A good communicator knows this and always tries to be a POSR. In other words, he or she always tries to:

Play

Off

Stored

Responses

Take a lawyer as storyteller, for example. Great litigators are always thinking about questions such as what kind of language and stories will work best in the jurisdiction in which they are practicing. What are the unconscious biases in their potential jurors? What's already in their audience's minds that they can play off of? What emotional baggage does each jury member bring to the room? And how do they use it or defuse it?

Great advertising and marketing executives do the same thing. They are always scrupulously studying their target markets and shaping their message for that audience. Know thy audience and how to speak to them, and you will surely succeed.

The same holds true for any good storyteller. You must always be conscious of your audience. You must always think about which words to use or not use. And you must always base the kind of stories you tell on your intended audience.

You can't just power through your story with the attitude "I am right and I know the truth, so I am going to force that truth on my audience, and they will completely accept it and love me, my product, and my story." Effective business people know to avoid that type of approach, no matter how compelling and intelligent the story might be.

The four Fs and IRMs

Although everyone has stored responses based upon their own personal experiences, we also have other human responses that are more intrinsic and hard-wired into our systems.

A good communicator and storyteller intuitively knows that people are driven by the four Fs: Food, Flight, Fight, and F—er, I mean, Procreation.

What you may not know is that we are also driven by Innate Releasing Mechanisms (IRMs). The four Fs are fairly self-evident, and I will not explain them, but IRMs are a little less known, so let me clarify what that term means.

In essence, an Innate Response Mechanism is an automatic response to something that we experience. For example, as I just mentioned, a person pulls back in fear and shudders when he or she hears a lion's roar or sees a snake for the first time. Our brains are more than just a bundle of learned responses; in some cases, the response is triggered by information that is hard-wired in our brains.

As a playwright, I have had the privilege of seeing this human hard-wiring in action. Whenever one of my plays is in production, I go to the theater and watch the audience watching my play. As I watch them, I learn a tremendous amount from their responses.

You see, the audience is always right. If their eyes are glazing over as they watch my play, I know I need to do a big edit and I need to do it fast. If it is a comedy and they aren't laughing, I know I have a long night ahead of rewrites that will include crafting a lot of new jokes until I get it right.

The same is true for all people seeking an audience, whether writer, actor, advertising executive, human relations personnel, or any businessperson. Your audience is never wrong in the sense that if they don't understand your story, it's not their fault. You simply need to revise your telling of the tale. Sure, it's the audience's job to listen and try to absorb, but it's your job as a storyteller to connect with them.

It's your job to tell such a gripping story that they want to listen to you. Ideally, each time you share something new, they can't wait for it to come out, because they know you are going to have something compelling to say and they want to listen to you.

This brings up an issue that I see with many of my clients. Is it up to us as the marketers to convince people of what they need, or do we have to respond to the needs of the consumers? I will once again refer to the wisdom of Bill Bernbach, who said, "We are so busy measuring public opinion that we forget that we can mold it.

We are so busy listening to statistics that we forget we can create them" (*www.azquotes.com/quote/684037*).

I love this quote because it empowers us to follow our marketing instincts. Statistics and marketing research are incredibly helpful tools, but they are not an end in themselves. They are merely a means to an end, which is the crafting of a powerful and effective message that will set you apart from all others!

Before we move on to other points, I feel compelled to share one more Bernbach quote: "Our job is to sell our clients' merchandise... not ourselves. Our job is to kill the cleverness that makes us shine instead of the product. Our job is to simplify, to tear away the unrelated, to pluck out the weeds that are smothering the product message" (*www.brainyquote.com/quotes/authors/w/william_bernbach.html*).

So, in the end, any good story, any good message, is less about you and more about your message and conveying it in a way that is fresh, original, and will stay with your customers.

Cool neurocognitive stuff

Ultimately, though, no matter whether we are reading a magazine, watching TV, or participating in a corporate meeting—in other words, no matter the venue—it is necessary to consider the nature of how humans store information once it's conveyed.

First, if one studies memory, learning, and neurocognitive theories, it becomes clear that information is costly to obtain, costly to store, and costly to retrieve. It is also clear that human memory is reconstructive and contextual. Thus, from a neurocognitive viewpoint, information that is contextually grounded will store more easily in human memory.

Because you are part of a business looking to increase your audience and to inspire deeper audience engagement, think about these claims in the context of marketing and sales. In the marketing text *Buying In*, by Rob Walker, the author aims to show how meaningful objects are rarely chosen through rational means and, instead, are chosen through narratives that we generate about ourselves in choosing a particular product. Walker says, "Successful brands are able to create some sort of meaning for consumers. The 'meaning' will have value depending on the person's experience with the brand, and if successful, the brand will hold value for that person throughout their life. It will come to *mean* something to them."

We can't help it. That's what we do; we write stories to endow our lives with meaning. We are story-driven creatures who even create narratives about inanimate objects such as cans of cola or bags of cheese puffs! And it is the well-told stories about these objects that stay with us way past the expiration date on the bottle or the bag.

Think about it. When you are walking down the supermarket aisle and are confronted with a wide array of breakfast cereals, why do you choose one box over another? Sure, there might be price-point issues, but let's say that if most of the bags are at similar price points, how does the average consumer differentiate?

Well, they unconsciously conjure stories in their heads of positive or negative experiences with the different brands and choose accordingly.

For example, I'm a Golden Grahams guy. The truth is that even though they seemingly purport to be a healthy breakfast cereal, Golden Grahams are as sugary as many of the other breakfast cereals, but I'm drawn to them because I spent many a happy day as a young man munching on them straight out of the box. Hence, when confronted with making a choice, without really thinking about it, I tend to go with the box that represents a return to the carefree and happy days of my youth.

The curse of bulleted copy

So now the next question arises. If stories are truly a powerful way to transmit information, why do so many people and companies rely on conveying essential brand information with bulleted copy and PowerPoint presentations?

PowerPoint is a technological advancement, but in terms of storytelling it could be interpreted as a step backward. PowerPoint's emphasis on bullet points, information dumping, diagrams, pie charts, and pyramids can be visual and effective, but these elements, by their very nature, might also make PowerPoint antithetical to the narrative impulse in all of us.

In fact, it might be argued that PowerPoint's greatest drawback is that it focuses the reader's attention on the screen and away from the person who is talking. By its very nature, PowerPoint defeats the core objective of any storyteller: to enhance the relationship with his or her audience. In doing so, it leads to disengagement instead of connection.

Furthermore, does the nature of PowerPoint force us to think only of the presentation we are working on in terms of short lists of facts? Does our thinking actually shrink to fit into the narrow parameters of a bullet list? And, in so doing, does it limit the way we look at a presentation and the potential stories we could tell in that presentation? Bulleted copy is antithetical to good storytelling. It might very well get in the way of your desired emotional impact. They have the potential to close down the imagination of your audience instead of opening and enlarging it.

- If we keep writing in bullet points,
- one day we will become automatons who
- talk and think in bulleted copy.

The brilliant strategy planner, Martin Weigel, pointed this out to me. The bullet point format works as a list and as a list, it is inherently limiting. Bulleted copy would have ruined all of the great speeches of the past. This is a function of the fact that great speeches have an emotional content that bullet points can't contain. Beyond the physical presentation of the speech, the content is more than something that can be boiled down to several bullet points.

Can bulleted copy convey Martin Luther King, Jr.'s sentiments about creating a better society in his "I Have a Dream" speech? What about Lincoln's Gettysburg Address? The information in it could be placed in bullet points, but what kind of effect on his audience do you think that would have had?

When you have a big presentation for clients, consumers, or shareholders, will a PowerPoint deck be able to convey the emotional message that you need to get across in order to keep your job and woo your audience? Can bulleted copy ever be as equally inspiring as a heartfelt story told well and in your own voice?

As I was writing this section of the book, I took a break to check my e-mail and I saw a pop-up ad about Heinz Ketchup, one of my all-time favorite products. I have tried many types of ketchup, but I am a believer in Heinz. I love the consistency and taste of this product and can't imagine eating fries or a hot dog or hamburger without it. I have been pouring bottle after bottle of their ketchup onto my meals since I was a little kid. Time and time again, people have made snide comments to me such as, "Hey, condiment boy, gonna put some french fries on that ketchup?"

And when I saw the Heinz ad, I couldn't help but smile due to all the good associations that I have with their products. So, I decided to explore further. The ad mentioned a happiness contest Heinz was sponsoring.

Wonderful. Heinz Ketchup makes me happy when I eat and so I was motivated to explore and learn more. I assumed that Heinz was trying to emotionally differentiate themselves from their competitors by owning the emotional landscape of happiness. *Good idea*, I thought. I eagerly clicked the link and waited to see what would happen next.

The link was broken. Not good. Then I entered the Heinz.com Web address into my browser and got to their Website. Once there, I double-clicked on "Our Company" and I was taken to a page that looked like the following (this has been edited for brevity's sake, but I just wanted to give you an idea of it):

Heinz at a Glance

- Heinz was founded in Sharpsburg
- Heinz products enjoy #1 or #2 market share...
- Heinz's top 15 power brands account for...
- Heinz sells 650 million bottles of its iconic Ketchup every year
- Heinz is a responsible corporate citizen...

Now, all of this information about Heinz sounds good, but cumulatively, this type of bulleted copy has very little long-term impact on me as a consumer. It feels cold and, frankly, all a bit off-putting. It seems to be antithetical to the brand and the core concept of happiness.

On the opposite side of the Web page, however, there is more of a compelling story. If you go to the Website, you will see a story about Heinz and Home. It tells of Heinz's passion for good food and how Heinz knows that you care about nutrition and your loved ones. It talks about not settling for anything less than the highest quality food and how Heinz has been part of families for more than 100 years. Then, it ends with an invitation to discover more about Heinz.

This is much better. Not a fully realized, emotionally moving story yet, but at least there are seeds of some emotional material here. I think there is potential in this idea of home and family to create some truly stirring brand narratives that would lead to much further engagement and connection with consumers. As well, it would help both the Heinz brand and consumers get closer to happiness.

In addition, I watched their corporate video, and it is clear Heinz is doing wonderful things to help starving children and the environment, but this also did not come through in their bulleted copy.

So, you need to be very careful with the use of bulleted copy and consider re-evaluating how you think of PowerPoint and how it should be used in your presentations. What if your next PowerPoint presentation merely used a series of forceful, image-based demonstratives without words? What if you provided the voiceover and let your stories resonate with your audience as beautiful images played in front of their eyes?

Or what if you turned off the projector altogether and just told a story about your next product—without any visual aids at all except the imagination of your audience?

It would seem revolutionary, even though it's what people were doing in corporate boardrooms and sales meetings for hundreds of years before they had laptops or digital projectors.

You don't have to spend your life as a bulleted copy automaton. You can quickly start to rethink PowerPoint as just one of many tools you can use to tell powerful, persuasive stories to your staff and potential hires, or to your clients/customers and potential clients/customers.

Prioritize your story and its theme, and watch how everything else will follow. And if you really take these precepts to heart, you might even be able to rewrite the story of your future and the future of your story.

I am not saying that you should never use bulleted copy again, but please use it judiciously. When you do use it, think about employing it to serve a higher purpose—that of the larger story and theme of your message.

Think about the nature of every slide. Does every slide have tons of information dumped onto it? You might think this is a good thing, but it's difficult to process; thus, instead of engaging, it alienates your audience!

Does your slide have a good image on it? All slides should have a visual component that makes them appealing.

Does your slide have less than seven words on it? Less is more. You should never just read your slides. Instead, use them as a springboard for your discussion. Remember: You don't want your audience paying too much attention to your slides. You want your audience paying attention to your message!

Does your slide ask a good question so that your audience needs to listen to you to get the answer? The slide should provoke thought and the desire for more information and clarification. It is this query that leads the audience to listen to you, the presenter, to get the goods, the solution, and the answer!

The Golden Rule of Storytelling

It should be pretty clear by now that a list of information or, for that matter, bullet points without stories and characters, has no emotional resonance and, thus, will not be very well remembered by your audience.

Instead, to more deeply connect with potential customers, please consider following Professor K.'s Golden Rule of Storytelling—a tool I've shared with my students and audiences for decades to help ensure storytelling success. It is simply this:

An engaging character
actively overcomes
tremendous obstacles
to reach a desirable goal,
and in doing so, the character changes for the better.

This is the goal of all stories. This is the gold standard. This is the ideal that all your brand narratives should aspire to.

You need to tell a story about engaging characters overcoming tremendous obstacles to reach desirable goals and hopefully, along the way, changing for the better. (And the bigger and more daunting the obstacle, the more compelling the story becomes.)

If you do this well, your audience will remember your story and you. After having consulted using this golden rule with novelists on 500-page books, with lawyers on three-hour courtroom presentations, and with marketing execs on 30-second TV commercials, I know that, regardless of the time you have to convey your story, it can be done.

Through the course of this little primer, I will give you a series of examples in which I will show how this Golden Rule of Storytelling is universal. All the various companies I've worked with have employed it with a variety of consumer products—everything from soap and shampoo to sneakers and bread.

So, rather than simply discussing how your products or services are cost-effective or eco-friendly or technologically advanced, consider telling specific stories of consumers whose lives were transformed by your products or services.

If you do that successfully, we—your audience—will care about you. We will create an emotional connection to you in the same way that a sports team creates an emotional bond with its loyal fans or a great restaurant creates a connection with its most fanatical patrons.

This is a viable, achievable goal if the right stories about you are told well and shared via the right communication channels. A well-orchestrated, systematic program of stories and messages told by you can literally change the way the world looks at you, your brand, and your company.

Before we end this chapter, I want to share a recent conversation I had with PR and marketing executive Kathy Copas about brand narratives today. Here are some of her thoughts:

RK: How do you see brand narratives today?

KC: I think the one thing we see pretty consistently in consumer behavioral research is that, in our increasingly fragmented society, what people are most seeking is an intangible called affiliation. That sense of affiliation, of relational connection with like-minded others, can most authentically and readily be achieved through story.

RK: How do you create brand narratives, especially in regards to social media?

KC: Calling forth those significant daily common life experiences via social media can both reveal and enhance brand identity. I like to think of creating digital narrative as shaping and stoking a virtual fireplace—a place to sit in a circle with others, swap stories, and reveal common humanity in a way that it leads to genuine personal feelings of affiliation with both product and product supporters. Once that sense of affiliation really catches fire, it will burn brightly and effectively with even occasional tending.

RK: Can marketers control brand narratives?

KC: I think presuming that any marketer can truly control how consumers alter brand narratives in this climate is naive. What an effective marketer or communicator *can* do is craft an effective space for brand narrative to naturally emerge.

RK: How would you define brand narratives?

KC: I would define brand narratives as positive product truths that are uncovered and nourished by cultivating genuine consumer affiliation with the product, as well as relationships with kindred users of that product.

RK: Can you talk about what kind of brand narratives you think are most effective?

KC: Stories of how a product or service positively and specifically impacted everyday life—that's an obvious one. Stories
of universal human experience. Stories of connection, of
how a product/experience built affiliation with others and
helped them to feel a part of something beyond themselves. Stories of transformation: illness to health, want
to abundance, isolation to inclusion, despair to hope, and
illumination of other basic aspirational human themes.

RK: Can you talk about how you think brand narratives have
changed in the age of digital communication and social
media?

KC: It is more about effectively uncovering the narrative from
your current consumers, making it easy and even fun for
them to share, craft, and own their message about why
your product is different/better than a comparable competitor's product. This is the only curation of message that
has integrity for your potential customers. Anything else
in this climate is just seen as unseemly, suspicious, and
top-down. A big part of what you are doing with your
curation of message in today's climate is dismantling any
hierarchical sense of selling, which is why uncovering and
purveying genuine story is still so effective.

RK: Do you have a specific process in which you craft brand
narratives?

KC: That would vary, depending on the product, service, or situation. But, I think the best brand narratives emerge naturally from product or service users. Sometimes, our very
best strategy is simply to create and nurture the virtual
fireplace for swapping stories and get out of the way and
watch/listen for the most effective and real narratives to
take shape. Then, we most authentically become carriers
of story, purveyors of brand truths, as opposed to marketers attempting to sell.

> —Kathy Copas, owner of Communication Services
> in New Albany, Indiana

CHAPTER 4

The Brand Narrative Manifesto

IIIIIIIIIIIIIIIIIIIIIIIIIIIIIIIIIIIIIIIIIIIIIIIIIIIIIIIIIIIIIIIIIIIIIIIIIIIIIIIIIIIIIIIIIIIIIIIIIIIIIIIIIIIIIIIIIIIIIIIIIIIIIIIIIIIIIIII

It will be no longer enough to produce a useful product. A story or legend must be built into it, a story that embodies values beyond utility. What is happening now is that the story that shapes our feelings about a product has become an enormous part of what we buy when we buy a product.
—Rolf Jenson, *The Futurist*

Let us now go deeper and really explore and think about why people buy things and the specific stories that play a role in the decisions that consumers are constantly making. Why do we choose to buy what we buy? What really drives those decisions and what role does narrative play in such decisions?

Let me try to answer some of those questions now. First of all, most people blame marketing for something it isn't responsible for at all. They say things like "Our marketing isn't bringing in any sales." Well, marketing isn't charged with bringing in sales. The sales function is responsible for making sales. The purpose of marketing is to support sales by, first and foremost, communicating differentiation and compelling storytelling, building brand presence, and creating opportunities for the sales function to close deals.

There is an age-old formula for this called AICP. Every person goes through this process when making a purchase.

Awareness.

Interest.

Consideration.

Purchase.

Differentiation is vital. I often do this simple test with new clients: I'll take their ad, brochure, or any literature, and place their competitor's logo over theirs. Then, if the claims on the literature also apply and are valid for the competition, it's clear that they are not sufficiently differentiated. And if a company is not sufficiently differentiated, a potential sales prospect really has nothing of value to use when they are making a purchasing choice.

A brand narrative manifesto

If you ask people why they chose a certain product, service, candidate, or team, they might try to give you a sensible, logical rationale.

"It was cheaper."

"It looked better."

"She has the right qualifications to lead this city."

"They've got a top-notch coach."

But the real reasons people make those kinds of choices go beyond these answers. For many of the products and services consumers buy, as well as for many of the things they buy into, other more subtle rationales are at work.

The days of differentiating a product or brand by function and/ or price are over. You can't merely say, "We're different because we're a little cheaper," or "We're better because we look at our special organic molecules." That kind of copy just doesn't cut it with the consumer who has seen it all and heard it all.

Take an old friend of mine who was a farmer in the Deep South. He is an inveterate Coca-Cola drinker and wouldn't drink Pepsi even if it was half the price of Coke. When I asked him about this preference, he told me, "Pepsi'll give you stomach problems. I know people who've gotten stomach cancer from drinking it."

I then offered him a Mountain Dew. And he said, "No, sir. You can't trick me. That's a Pepsi product and I won't touch it."

So what exactly is going on here? I have to admit, I was a bit confused by this at first. But then I looked at his history. He's a Georgia native who grew up 80 miles from Atlanta, home of Coca-Cola. He was raised in an environment where nobody drank Pepsi. All of his fondest childhood memories have a bottle or can of Coke in them. All of his family reunions feature only one kind of soft drink; take a guess at what it might be. You got it: Coke!

If you think about it, people buy things for emotional benefits, for security, to express themselves, to feel good, to show how unique they are, to feel connected with others, and for many other essentially subconscious reasons. But all these add up to one real reason: People buy things to give their life greater meaning.

Many intangible factors—such as memories, the rumored or real behavior of the company that produces the product, the fact-based or erroneous opinions of others, even the consumer's true or false conceptions about the product—all end up having a huge impact on what that person purchases and on brand loyalty.

Remember all the ruckus about Nike hiring children in foreign lands to make their sneakers? Even though it's been years since Nike rectified this, I know people who, today, still won't buy any Nike products.

Emotional differentiation

A brand with a price advantage can simply be undercut. A brand with a performance advantage can be outflanked by technological development. But a brand with an emotional difference can potentially command a premium forever.
        —Don Cowley, *Understanding Brands*

In a media-saturated world where the average consumer is bombarded with thousands of messages a day, how do you create an authentic emotional response, especially when consumers are so jaded, busy, and overwhelmed?

Think of it this way: If products are things without emotions, then the brand is the emotional beating heart of the product. It is only through stories, through brand narratives, that it is possible to create an emotional relationship between people and brands, thereby connecting them. This is what I like to call "emotional differentiation."

In other words, people buy things because of the emotional meaning or advantage that thing provides them. Tell a good story about your brand that provides a compelling emotional feeling and guess what they will do when they have to choose between products in the supermarket aisle.

In essence, an engaging brand narrative will circumvent our defenses and slip through to reach the deepest parts of ourselves. So, if you can create well-executed, on-target brand narratives, you will have tremendous power. You can foster word of mouth, brand loyalty, and maybe even brand advocacy.

Please note: Emotional differentiation is significant in any brand narrative, but it tends to be more prevalent with brands that are in well-known and crowded markets. In other words, if you are introducing the first MP3 player on the market, then you need to tell a knowledge-based story that gives the consumer tremendous information about the functions (and benefits) of the product.

However, if you are introducing a new MP3 player 10 years after they have saturated the market, you need not tell people about the functions of an MP3 player. In that case, you need only to emotionally differentiate how your new MP3 player stands apart from all the others out there. Consumers already know what MP3 players do. Now, they only need to know how yours is different.

Here's another example. If you are introducing the first cola in the marketplace, you need to let people know about the taste and qualities of a cola-flavored soft drink. However, if, as is the case today, people already know everything they need to know about what a cola is, you need only to differentiate this product emotionally.

Think about it. What is Coke advertising today? The brand's ads don't deal with Coke's flavor or its price point; instead, they seem to focus on happiness. And Pepsi is also not talking about price or taste, but instead seems focused on the energy of youth. So I think it's fair to argue that Coke is attempting to own the emotion of happiness while Pepsi is attempting to own the youth-oriented emotions.

And now, one more story

I have a friend whose wife loves jewelry. She really loves jewelry. And, fortunately for him, it's not the gold and diamond kind but the silver and semi-precious gem kind, which is less expensive.

A few years ago, he discovered a wholesale, discount semi-precious gem and silver jewelry store in Manhattan that carries the exact kind of pieces she loves. So he knew what to do every time her birthday or their anniversary came around.

Of all the gifts he'd gotten her there, her all-time favorite was a silver link chain bracelet set with at least 20 large, raw ruby-red gemstones. Every time she wore it, she got a big kick out of seeing all the deep, dark scarlet stones sparkle on her wrist.

All was good in their world until she came home from work one day only to discover that one of the gemstones had fallen out of its setting. Gone! Vanished! Lost forever!

Because her husband had purchased it for her, he was enlisted to hand-deliver it back to the jeweler and get it fit with a new matching stone. He did as instructed upon his next trip to the Big Apple.

Time passed. Life went on, and in the daily fray, they forgot about the bracelet. Then, a week before he had a meeting scheduled in Manhattan, he turned to her and said, "You know, I've got a meeting in the city. If you want me to pick up your ruby bracelet, I can."

She instantly responded, "Yes, definitely. If you don't mind."

He called the jeweler and told him, "I'll be in the city in a few days, and my wife wants me to pick up her favorite bracelet."

After a brief silence, the jeweler said, "Sir, I think I returned that to you."

"Oh no, my wife said you still have it."

There was a long pause. Finally, the jeweler answered, "Well, um, I could be wrong. Let me look. Maybe my repair guy still has it."

This was not good. My friend did not have a receipt, and he could tell the jeweler had no idea where the bracelet was. He pushed the jeweler further by asking, "Well, I'm only going to be in the city for one day, and my wife is dying to get the bracelet back. So, if I take a cab over there, will you definitely have it ready for me?"

"Yes, of course, sir," the jeweler said. "Don't worry about it. I promise it will be here when you come by."

The following week my friend dropped by the jewelry store. When he walked in, the jeweler smiled and handed him the bracelet. My friend flew home that night and gave it to his wife.

She was thrilled. She couldn't even tell which ruby was the one he had replaced. Before she went to sleep that night, she wanted to store it somewhere safe, so she went to put it in her jewelry box only to find that her repaired ruby bracelet was already there, hidden under another bracelet in the back of the box!

Yes, a few months earlier, their jeweler had indeed sent it back to her. My friend's wife had received it, and in order to ensure it was safe, she had immediately put it in her jewelry box and forgotten all about it.

My friend and his wife both felt pretty stupid. He immediately called the jeweler and apologized profusely. The next morning, my friend FedExed the duplicate bracelet back to the jeweler.

The jeweler admitted he knew from the moment my friend had called him that he had already fixed and returned the bracelet. But when my friend insisted he hadn't, the jeweler had made a new one for him without charging him, just to make sure he didn't lose a good customer.

My friend was blown away by this level of customer service, and from that moment on, he was a customer for life. And you better believe that when he talks about shopping in New York City, he always tells this story about the little shop with its amazing customer service!

And if you don't believe this story, just go to AF Jewelry on Broadway and 29th Street in New York City and ask for Wahid!

Activating passion on a mass scale

This tale of the ruby-red bracelet is a good example of how stories work, of how, in a consumer service industry, you can create faithful ambassadors for your brand. Engage people with extraordinary customer service, get them to start telling the world stories about your fantastic customer care, and just sit back and watch as customers convert to fans.

And, if you keep it up, within a few years you should have a cadre of loyal, passionate "sneezers" (my favorite term for brand ambassadors), who broadcast your brand's virtue to the world.

But what's really going on here under the surface? How do you explain and define my friend's conversion from customer to crusader? I would argue that the answer is this: Passion emanates from a positive interaction. The memorable emotive experience gives birth to the faithful ambassador who enthusiastically spreads the story about your brand to the world. A positive experience is transformed by a person into a positive story and, once told, that story spreads like wildfire in the form of good word of mouth. Think of it as the word of mouth form of viral videos. And no advertising dollars were spent in the process. Yep, it's every store-owner's dream.

And, in these days of diminishing product differentiation and of customers with little time and desire to sift through mountains of information to select the best product, this emotional bond can separate one brand from another and build long-term loyalty.

In essence, sometimes consumers buy your product not because of what you do, but because of why and how you do it. In other words, they buy because of your *story*.

How does all this translate to both large and small companies? It's essentially the same thing. In order to create a cult-like passion for their company and their products on a national level, every company, big or small, must create a brand narrative. And this company story should include product stories that share the same essential core message and theme.

How brand narratives work

Powerful, persuasive narratives are transformational. They are emotionally compelling. They are road maps for human growth and change. We are moved by the metamorphosis of the character in the narrative. As a result, we vicariously grow, learn, and change along with them.

This is what stories do. This is why we are drawn to them. This is why we remember them. Stories structure information into a coherent whole. In this era of PowerPoint, it is still stories that stay with us. It is their underlying values and our emotive response to those values that we, as consumers, retain. We remember a film that made us cry or a TV show that made us laugh. For example, as a teenager, I spent many a night watching reruns of *The Honeymooners* with my father and the two us laughing at Art Carney and Jackie Gleason. We shared our love for that show and those characters and, in doing so, it brought us closer together.

Stories work because in listening to or watching a well-told story, we are not outsiders. We are drawn in. In a brilliant play, we cross the threshold of the stage and become the hero. In a great novel, we dive into the text and become the protagonist. In an excellent film, we jump through the screen and disappear into the scene. In a good ad, we are transported from our reality into the brand's reality.

Narratives have a vicarious power. This has been demonstrated in a series of recent neurocognitive studies about the nature of brain chemistry. The research shows that in terms of chemical reactions in the brain, there's no difference between riding a roller coaster that goes out of control and watching a movie about someone who rides a roller coaster that goes out of control. In both situations, the same chemical response occurs in the amygdala in the temporal cortex. The brain doesn't have the ability to differentiate between virtual and actual.

Mirror neurons and you

This concept is further reinforced by the idea of "mirror neurons," which was first postulated by Dr. Giacomo Rizzolatti. Mirror neurons allow us to mentally mirror, or duplicate, the actions of others. This concept becomes even clearer when we think about how children learn. They watch, hear, and mimic. They are able to do this because of the mirror neurons in the brain that fire based upon certain exterior cues.

What does this mean in terms of storytelling? Well, if you think about it, reading about or hearing a story or watching it on screen can activate the mirror neurons. When this happens, we will have an empathetic response, and if what we are hearing or watching is compelling, we will feel a bond or connection with the story and the elements within the story.

Go to a movie theater and, instead of watching the movie itself, watch the audience watch the movie. If you do, you will see mirror neurons in action. Movies have been constructed to take advantage of this human dependency on mirror neurons. We respond physically to images on screen as if they are real. As a species, we evolved this way to help us survive. It is tied into the evolutionary benefit of compassion. If we feel for others, we will help them and, as a result, we will continue the species. (Obviously, we also do things to hinder the species, but that is a longer conversation.)

As a social species, mirroring probably aided survival in a few different ways. First, it helped develop coordinated action among groups. Like a child that mimics a parent, an apprentice can mimic his master and learn a craft. Wouldn't a species benefit from learning from other successful members of that species? If the brain is constructed with a neural pathway that allows for easy imitation, doesn't this aid in learning?

So, you are sitting in a movie theater watching people watching the film on screen. What do they do? Well, when characters cry on screen, what happens in the theater? And what about laughter? During an action scene, do people tense up or relax? There is even an imitating of facial expressions that occurs.

In Jeffrey Zacks's excellent book on mirroring and the movies, *Flicker: Your Brain on Movies*, he cites an interesting study: "In one study conducted at the University of Indiana in the 1960s, researchers asked people to listen to jokes either alone or in groups. The group audiences laughed more. Interestingly, they didn't rate the jokes as any funnier; perhaps they laughed more not because they thought the jokes were any funnier, but as a direct result of seeing or hearing their fellow audience members yukking it up."

This explains things like laugh tracks and why funny movies seem funnier in a theater filled with laughing people versus an empty theater. If your video is working well with audiences, it will trigger their mirror neurons and you will be making a real connection with your desired audience, one that will stay with them for longer than the 20 or 30 seconds the spot takes to run. In the workshops that I provide, the executives I work with have a chance to see this in action. They write stories and test them on each other, measuring and re-adjusting their stories so as to gauge what resonates, as well as what is retained and what isn't.

In other words, new systems of meaning can be created through emotional brand narratives. Thankfully, one of the most opportune repercussions of our new media-saturated society is that there are tons of opportunities for storytellers, and even consumers themselves, to create new stories that can be shared across the total brand communication platform. With an understanding of mirror neurons, of the human tendency toward empathy and sociability, we should be able to see the rise of new "tribal" formations.

A vicarious leap to a new emotional era

These days, in many product categories, there isn't a vast difference between products. Most skin care creams do essentially the same thing. Is one box of laundry detergent really that much different than another?

Product differentiation is hard to achieve, let alone sustain. As a result, marketing has been forced to move beyond functional differentiation to an era of emotional differentiation. Marketers must touch the emotions of consumers; they must find a new place in the consumers' hearts.

In this era of emotions, values-based differentiation makes *story* central, because this is exactly what narratives can do and have done for millennia. Basically, brand narratives work by activating emotions and communicating values.

Instead of hitting us on the head with a message, stories convey information by teaching and entertaining. They work best when they are edu-tainment!

If a national brand can't interact directly with consumers as a result of their size, the brand can at least interact vicariously with consumers via stories, via brand narratives created for traditional and nontraditional media outlets. Any company creating a brand or further developing an established brand can determine the values with which they want to be aligned.

Companies can communicate those specific values through carefully constructed, highly engaging brand narratives and then deliver them to consumers via a variety of forms of media.

In the same way that my friend's jeweler created a deep emotional bond with my friend through extraordinary customer service, a brand has the opportunity to build an emotional bond with millions of consumers through its extraordinary brand narratives. This, then, is my clarion call for compelling, engaging brand narratives.

From preference to passion

When you learn how to tell moving, personal brand stories and to tell them so well that you consistently evoke the desired emotive response, you can achieve the same thing as the New York City jeweler did when he turned my friend into a customer for life. And you can do it on a mass scale.

You can create passionate customers who, when they see your brand, will remember a story they saw that your brand told on the Internet, in print, or on TV. Then, they might also remember a personal story dealing with how they interacted with your brand. For instance, do you remember your favorite brand of candy or ice cream as a kid?

Let's say your brand is Breyers Ice Cream Company. Your loyal customers might remember being a child and having their mothers serve them a bowl of your ice cream to help them feel better, thus aligning your brand with a positive, nurturing emotive memory. As a result, the consumers' own stories become intertwined with the Breyers' brand narratives, and you move from being an impersonal corporate brand to a close, personal ally.

So think deeply about the brand narratives that already exist with consumers as well as the brand narratives that are being created every day. Much can be learned from both, and both also have tremendous potential power.

Because storytelling can be taught, we can and should try to master the rules and tools that will allow us to make compelling narratives. We can then use those rules and tools to create emotionally engaging stories. And then we can broadcast those narratives to consumers via traditional and new media to provide them with the emotive experiences that lead to brand passion.

Through the power of stories, we can make the leap from preference to passion—and maybe even to love.

Now, let's talk to Katja Bressette, consumer researcher, psychologist, and consultant about her take on brand narratives:

RK: What role do you see storytelling playing in branding and marketing today?

KB: It is essential. A brand or a product needs to tell a compelling, engaging story in order to be heard, to resonate, to have an impact. It is so important because storytelling is a powerful way humans make sense of the world, convey information, learn, and connect with others (this includes people and brands).

RK: How do you create, cultivate, and sustain life long relationships with customers via digital narratives across all forms of media?

KB: Life long is ambitious in this day and age! First, you have to deeply understand your customers and understand the frames that impact what they hear and how they act. These frames could be archetypes; they could be the Deep Metaphors Jerry Zaltman has made so prominent; they could be another framework based in psychology, behavioral sciences, etc. Using this as a foundation, you can create narratives in and for various formats and media that activate and tap into these guiding frames. And you have to account for change—in the marketplace, in consumers' minds, brands. Nothing is forever, not even the deepest framework and certainly not the different kinds of media and devices.

RK: It is said that it is not just about storytelling anymore, but about timeless, ever-evolving brand narratives that you must create and control. Do you agree and, if so, can you comment?

KB: Of course. Brand narratives must evolve and change (and they do, whether marketers want to or not); the market, consumers, brands, products evolve. External factors impact all four, such as an economic downturn (which can have a huge impact on consumer narratives), political changes, world events, new technologies or brands (for example, think what Tesla is doing to the automotive industry and their narratives), cohort changes/development (Boomers are still very much running the show, but for how much longer?), etc.

Can you ever completely control all aspects of these narratives? I do not think so. However, marketer-created frames/stories/meaning blend with those of consumers and, together, you co-create the narrative as it exists in consumers' minds. For that reason, you cannot control, but you can understand consumers' frames and the resulting co-creation with your story, and out of that develop and create ongoing, compelling narratives. You can even include consumers in that process and, in doing so, further the agenda of your own narratives.

RK: Marketing used to be about creating a myth and selling it; now it is about finding a truth and sharing it. We are moving from storytelling to brand narratives. So what exactly are brand narratives?

KB: For me, brand narratives represent a move away from the "broadcasting" model of marketing (a brand/product sends out a story/myth/meaning and expects consumers to be passive receivers who can just be injected with that story) to a digital/interactive model of constant co-creation. Brand narratives are a two-way street and the narrative includes both consumer and brand stories/meaning/myths.

Experiences are very important in brand narratives. Narratives are the result of not just communication efforts but, perhaps even more so, experiences with a brand or product. Therefore, inspiring consumers to have experiences with a brand or product or utilizing experiences they are already having is very powerful. Kleenex Canada's Share the Care is a beautiful example.

RK: Do you have a specific process in which you craft brand narratives that you would be willing to share with readers?

KB: I mainly utilize online mobile ethnography, mixed with other proven tools to uncover consumers' stories, frames, meaning, and behavior patterns. For example, I might include a psychological assessment to uncover consumers' core personality and characteristics, projective exercises to uncover brand and consumer archetypes, and, of course, mobile ethnography. The videos and images created by consumers give an incredibly powerful and compelling view into their minds and, with that, the stories and myths around a brand/product/experience. And they provide a springboard from which to probe more deeply into their experiences, emotions, beliefs, and specific stories. Out of this, I create the consumer story, which includes guiding frames (for example, archetypes or simple models), behavior patterns, guiding emotions, consumer personality, etc. In the implications section, I make suggestions for resonating brand narratives and brand experiences. Experiences, after all, lead to stories: stories in our minds and stories we tell others. And if the experiences and stories are positive, they can indeed lead to lifelong loyalty. Think about your favorite brands or products. I am sure there is a great story behind your love for/connection to them.

—Katja E. Bressette, MBA, MSW, founder/owner of
Beacon Insight Group

Part 2: Narrative Fundamentals

CHAPTER 5

Your Brand DNA

|||||||||||||||||||||||||||||||||||||||||||||||||||||||||||||||||||||||||||||||||||||||||||||||||||||||||||||||||||||||||||||||||||||||||||||||||||||||||||||||

God made humans because God loves stories.
— Chassidic proverb

Your story must be in line with your Brand DNA or it will be working against you. So really, what is Brand DNA?

The letters "DNA" are an acronym for deoxyribonucleic acid, which contains the core biological information that makes one species different from another. It is the hereditary material in humans and almost all other organisms. Nearly every cell in a person's body has the same DNA structure and, essentially, it is that which makes you you, and similar to, but still different from, other people.

When designing a project, the gifted architect Mark Knauer explores Brand DNA "Differences, Nature, and Attributes." In application to creating a brand narrative, Brand DNA forms the core of what you want your message to be. It is the essence of what makes your brand different from all others. It should be expressed in as few words or phrases as possible, and they must be words or phrases that epitomize your business's soul. These key words and phrases then drive all stories told about the business throughout the marketing process.

Just as biological DNA determines what characteristics a person has in their genetic makeup, Brand DNA determines what attributes are "baked into" a business. Key words and phrases are chosen carefully to represent the very essence of the genetic code of the business. Every decision about business brand issues will be influenced by referring to and adhering to this Brand DNA.

By properly utilizing Brand DNA as a tool, concepts will evolve and become fortified, resulting in a richer, more clarified version of the business.

Once you determine the core essence of what is and what isn't in your Brand DNA, you need to then consider your brand and product's role in the life of consumers and the appropriate direction for your narratives. There are way too many examples of companies that have not understood this and told the wrong story, which ended up hurting their brand. The most prominent example that comes to mind is a famous sneaker retailer that spent millions on a Super Bowl TV commercial that featured one of their Caucasian employees chasing a barefoot African runner. Once the barefoot runner was captured, the shoe salesperson gave him a brand new pair of branded sneakers and supposedly helped him.

The problem was that instead of gaining sales, the commercial, which was seen by millions and millions of people, did terrible harm to the brand. It was considered to be blatantly offensive by people of color. Many public watchdog groups also labeled it as imperialistic and offensive. The white salesperson capturing the barefoot black man did not play well with any of the targeted audiences. The story itself was not inherently poorly constructed, per se. It was the way the DNA of the story, the theme, associations, and meaning of it, were perceived by an audience that was harmful.

Your story has power. That power can essentially be used for good or evil. You need to consider how your story will affect your brand and how the wrong story can do more damage than good. So be careful. Take the time to truly determine your Brand DNA. Then take even more time to make sure that your brand narratives are all in line with that DNA, thus ensuring all of your stories help further your best identity.

Another issue that arose when constructing brand narratives with companies was that many of them tended to make the brand or the star product the hero of the brand narrative. This comes through in print ads, video, or Internet content where stories are shared that show the product saving the day. Hurray for my special soap or sweet soda that is so spectacular it changes the lives of everyone who uses or consumes it."

In other words, let's feature stories of how our product is so spectacular. This is tempting, but can also be dangerous. Your brand or product can be life altering, but you need to downplay it, or there is a very real chance that your brand narrative will push away consumers instead of pulling them in.

This was clearly illustrated to me when I was working in the haircare realm. The scripts coming my way kept showing miraculous transformations occurring as the result of women using a new bottle of shampoo. It was just too unbelievable and, as a result, I feared it would do more harm than good to the brand. The traditional before-and-after brand spot that I kept seeing over and over again felt problematic. In other words, I feared that the standard spot of a woman with bad hair who then uses the product and *poof,* instantly gains fantastic hair just lacks credibility today.

A truth became apparent to me. The brand in modern brand narratives couldn't be the hero. You can't just use a product and, overnight, be transformed by it and still be plausible. Instead, the brand/product must work as a helpful ally, not a miraculous hero.

What your product must do is work as a helpful ally that improves the life of the individual who needs it. So, let's take our shampoo again. Using a great new haircare product doesn't miraculously transform you into a different human being; instead, it allows you to feel better about yourself, and as a result, to achieve what you might not have been able to achieve without good hair. Your hair looks and smells good. Your shampoo as a helpful ally has allowed you to feel better about yourself and now you are more confident and, hence, better equipped to take on the difficulties of the day.

You do not have superpowers, you are not Wonder Woman, but you are a bit more confident and capable as a result of your new helpful ally that has given you a special little boost.

The brand as mentor

Here is an interview with Joel Klettke, the business casual copywriter, who gives us his take on business narratives, the brand as mentor, not hero, and how good copy can use story to further the goals of the Brand DNA:

RK: How do you see the rise of storytelling in the digital age today?

JK: Well, you could have predicted the progression from a mile away. The online marketing world has been slowly plodding its way along a natural time line, from the early days spent invested in loopholes and "whatever works" (read: cheap, scalable spam), to starting to think about audiences (contextual keyword targeting), to placing intense importance on content (create things people want to consume, instead of vying for their click). And now, here we are, the era of "brand storytelling." It's an ancient concept, but a relatively new buzzword—at least in a digital marketing context.

RK: What do you see as the basic argument for brand storytelling today?

JK: If you poke around the Web, the basic argument in favor of brand storytelling goes a little bit like this (some liberties taken): "Storytelling is the most powerful force in our communication. From the moment we were hairy, hideous cavemen, we've used stories to pass on information, share values, evoke emotions, and entertain one another around the campfire cooking woolly mammoth (before the advent of the vegan diet, apparently). Stories are the emotional glue that connects you with your adoring audience. They help frame your brand in a memorable and favorable light, aligning you with the shared values of your customer."

RK: Why do you like using storytelling when you create content?

JK: Numerous studies show that stories are more persuasive to the human mind than cold, hard facts—mostly because they allow us to suspend expectations of reality. Stories are also far easier to remember than content without context or narrative; we grow up listening to stories and know the ol' story arc very well (from introduction to climax to resolution, and everything in between). It's familiar in all the right ways; it gives the writer or speaker access to the emotional parts of a person and opens more doors for connection than just hard facts or cold anecdotes.

RK: Why then, do you think, there is so much bad brand storytelling online and in social media?

JK: Well, we think we all know a good story when we hear one. But then, let me ask: How is it that something we grow up surrounded by and accustomed to hearing turns into a sloppy mess when we apply it to branding? I think this is the result of the fact that it is easy to get confused when telling stories. So there are three common mistakes that you must avoid when telling brand stories.

1. The brand is not the hero.

Every story shares some elements of plot—and every story has some sort of hero or protagonist at the center. When it comes to brand storytelling, your brand is not the hero. The story does not go, "And the corn niblets bravely fought off the dangers of heart disease with fervor and grace. Buy Green Giant!"

Here's the thing: Brand storytelling is not really about you. It's about what you help your customers accomplish and the values that underpin your existence.

Corn niblets are not a hero your audience cares about or can relate to. Even though *you* want to throw your brand front and center, storytelling is about the customer and what you can do for them. You are the "Mentor," the person or thing that makes achieving a goal and rising above challenges (the original refusal to a call/tests and enemies/central ordeal as found in Joseph Campbell's

Hero Journey paradigm) possible. When you tell the story of the customer, you're really telling your own.

2. Appealing to foreign or inconsistent values.

Every brand has a story; that "story" is the sum of the brand's values, promises, and attitudes. While we talk about storytelling as a format for content, there is also a greater narrative outside of the content: the real-world perceptions of who you are and what you stand for. Those values need to remain consistent over time, because they're what attracted your audience in the first place.

Remember that telling a story is about wrapping your audience up in the narrative. The moment you stomp on their values or create a world they don't want to live in, you've lost them.

3. Displaying unrelatable characters.

The audience must be able to connect with the characters in your story. To appeal to your audience, they must be able to engage to a credible story. Your audience must be able to see themselves in the story and, thus, it becomes believable with real emotions.

RK: So then, any final words on how people can tell a better brand story?

JK: You must account for the values, desires, and imagination of the customer. By trying to be the hero or wrestle away the imagination of an audience, you are actually tripping over yourself. The stories that come out of your brand need to be consistent with what your customers stand for. You need heroes they can believe in or see themselves as. You need problems that really exist and narratives that could actually take place and appeal to emotions and challenges we all know and understand.

—Joel Klettke, Freelance Copywriter and Conversion
Optimization Specialist at Business Casual Copywriting
@JoelKlettke, joel@businesscasualcopywriting.com

CHAPTER 6

Turning Your Brand DNA Into Your Brand Narrative

||||||||||||||||||||||||||||||||||||||||||||||||||||||||||||||||||||||||||||||||||||||||||||||||||||||||||||||||||||||||||||||||||||||||||||||||

*Storytelling reveals meaning without
committing the error of defining itself.*
—Hannah Arendt

Y ou are constantly telling stories about your business. Whether that story is told in a speech, in ordinary conversation with coworkers or customers, or on your Website, advertising, or packaging, your story is aligned with the public face of your company and it must be carefully crafted from your Brand DNA.

So, once you have a clearly delineated Brand DNA, you need to start creating narratives that embody it. Here is a proven methodology you might employ. And, of course, you can also invent your own methodology if you prefer. The key thing is not "mine vs. yours," but to understand your Brand DNA and then systematically create internal and external communication in the form of brand narratives that help disseminate the message of your brand.

Prof. K.'s brand narrative methodology

Once I've spent hours working with a brand team and everyone has approved the Brand DNA, we are ready to move into the dissemination process. Please note: You need universal, 100-percent buy-in of the Brand DNA before you can move forward. Any less can lead to problems down the road, both with team members and the message. Get everybody aboard and get them to buy in, and then later in the process, if they disagree with a brand narrative, you can always point to the Brand DNA and show how it is in keeping with the core essence of the brand, which they agreed upon.

Here's an outline of Prof. K.'s 7 Step Brand Narrative Creation Methodology:

Step 1—Brand DNA Creation.

Step 2—Logo/Image Ideation via Physical Metaphors.

Step 3—Story Brainstorming.

Step 4—Brand Narrative First Draft.

Step 5—Revision and Rewriting.

Step 6—Testing and Fine Tuning.

Step 7—Brand Narrative Fruition Across All Media.

Now, let me break this down further and provide an explanation of each step for you. First, we have *Step 1—Brand DNA Creation*, which I just covered in detail in the previous chapter. Next, we have *Step 2—Logo/Image Ideation via Physical Metaphors*.

What does this mean? Here are the specifics for you. In order to find a way to systematically differentiate a company and/or product and then navigate a course of action to communicate this differentiation, you need to start with a physical, concrete visual metaphor that embodies who you are in a single glance. Think in terms of a point of uniqueness that is mentioned in your Brand DNA and can be fleshed out in a simple image. This is you at a glance. This is your brand in concrete metaphor. I look at this image and I instantly get what you are about. I understand your brand just from this.

Once you have one or more images that you like, it's time to start doing some compelling storytelling; it's time to create a brand narrative that embodies your new meaning. Look at your Brand DNA and your physical logo/metaphor. What kind of story does it make you think of? What kind of story is begging to be told about you?

As I've already mentioned and will continue to discuss throughout this book, one cannot just think of a story, write it down, and be good to go. The development of a powerful brand narrative is a long, tedious process and one that encompasses the next four steps of my methodology: Story Brainstorming, Brand Narrative First Draft, Revision and Rewriting, and Testing and Fine-Tuning. So, let's look at these four now:

Step 3—Story Brainstorming. This step is rather self-explanatory, but it is important. To create fresh and exciting new brand narratives, an environment must be created in which anybody on the team can throw out any story idea without the fear of negative repercussions. My nickname for this step is the "Shit and Wit Session." In calling it this, I give everybody permission to come up with the shittiest stories possible. In other words, one must be allowed to say and try any and all stories, no matter how good or bad, and in doing so, they might just spur the team on to discovering a truly great narrative.

Step 4—Brand Narrative First Draft. When the team comes up with one or more brand narratives that everybody likes, it's time to flesh out the story. Note that when I mention this methodology, I constantly speak of teams, not individuals. Sure, an individual can engage and successfully execute this process, but I prefer engaging in this methodology with teams. This process works best with teams of knowledgeable, passionate individuals who know the brand and can work in concert to create a brand narrative that is more powerful than something that any one individual can come up with.

So, work together, release any judgment, and just create. Write a first draft, no matter how bad it seems, and get it out there on paper or on the computer screen. Finish it. Complete a first draft of a story with a beginning, middle, and end, no matter how good or bad.

Step 5—Revision and Rewriting. This can sometimes seem like an endless process, but it is a valid and necessary one. There is no right number of necessary revisions, but I always recommend sharing the story with all team members, assimilating their notes, and then sharing again. Do as many revisions as necessary until you get universal acceptance by all team members. Then, and only then, test the story with people outside of the team.

Step 6—Testing and Fine-Tuning. Hollywood does test screenings of all its films for a reason. No matter how hard you've worked on your story, you have to test it and then, as a result of that test, fine-tune it and test it again before you go out to the public with it. There is nothing to be ashamed of here. Stories have to be refined over and over again before they are ready for consumption.

Step 7—Brand Narrative Fruition Across All Media. This will be covered in detail several chapters later in this book, but for now, let me just say that it is about determining what forms that story should take—oral, print, video, online, internal, external, etc.—and then adapting the brand narrative to fit that form of media.

I have come to see through experience that the methodology of this seven-step process is incredibly applicable to far more than just marketing alone. The process has been used successfully in sales, manufacturing, problem-solving, and team building. Engaging in this process can work as an assessment tool for uncovering core issues, and then it helps users to navigate useable, practical solutions to problems that have arisen. It works in concert with human nature and provides a way for one's inner brilliance to flow outward instead of being suppressed. The outcomes from this process allow managers to stop draining their efforts on managing consequences and resolve issues once and for all, regardless of their category of work.

Ideally, anybody should be able to understand this methodology and employ it, but this is not a simplistic tool that anybody can just plug in. It helps to have an experienced facilitator to really work it properly—one that is outside of the team and can give objective feedback as the brand narrative is created, nurtured, and then executed across different media platforms. In most cases, at first, the facilitator is usually an outside consultant who comes in, facilitates, and, in doing so, also trains one or more in-house personnel to serve as facilitators for future sessions.

A case study: Pureffic Gourmet Foods

Pureffic Gourmet Foods is a new company that is creating specialty food specifically for the dysphagia market—those people who have problems with chewing and swallowing. Let's look at how I led their team on a brand narrative journey.

Step 1—Brand DNA Creation. We got out a white board and went a bit crazy, throwing out any and all ideas that came to mind. Here is a list of some of the ones that we wrote down as we progressed:

- Satisfying.
- Homemade.
- Empower.
- Kitchen.
- Gratify.
- Real food.
- Wholesome.
- Eating is beyond nutrition.
- Discovery and rediscovery.
- It's about taste, pleasure, family, texture, gratification, flavor, joy.
- Labeling.
- Patient centeredness.
- Patient satisfaction.
- Statistics.

We then worked through all these ideas to get to a core concept, the Brand DNA that we reduced down to three words—Pureffic's new slogan: *Rediscover Real Food.*

Step 2—Logo/Image Ideation via Physical Metaphors. Logos are a physical manifestation/embodiment of your company and, as such, are hugely important. What image do you want to come to mind when people think of you? And how does that image embody your

Brand DNA, your brand narrative, and the emotions you want to ally yourself with?

Hence, the logo is a huge step and should not be taken lightly. So, we now needed to throw around a lot more ideas in terms of physical metaphors that might help us to find the perfect logo/image for the company.

What are the physical images that might represent us? Here is some of our work that came out of our session:

- Fork.
- Plate with ribbon representing phase A.
- Black chalkboard.
- Banana.
- Apple.
- String of apples.
- Artichoke.
- Fruit and vegetable.
- Olive branch.
- Spatula.
- Mop.
- Fireplace.
- Chef's hat.
- Orange wedge.
- Mason jar.
- Kitchen table.
- Spoon.
- A four-item circle.
- Red.
- Stethoscope.
- Purple.
- Green.
- Yellow.

After we felt like we'd covered all that we could, we put our heads together and ended up with a new logo that is basically the following: a brown stethoscope, a green fork, a red spatula, and a yellow banana rolled together into a circle with the name "Pureffic" in the center of that circle.

Step 3—Story Brainstorming. We discussed all the different stories that we could associate with the brand. Here are some ideas we came up with:

- An animated video: imagine a plate with good food on it that comes out of the oven, gets eaten, and all that is left are a few crumbs. Then, a mouse appears and eats the last crumbs. Then, our four physical metaphors come out one by one to form the logo.
- No matter what, they need to be emotional stories.
- A story with a family, the product user, and his or her caregivers.
- What are the best locations for our stories?
- A story about who we are.
- A story about how much money we want and why we need it (90 seconds).
- Caregiver story (60 seconds).
- User story (60 seconds).
- A doctor story (3 minutes).
- A technical aspect of our product story.
- A scene with everyone eating real food and a dysphagic eating horrible mush.
- A doctor explaining all the phases of our food and its labeling and all natural ingredients.
- Everyone sitting around table, shouting "Rediscover real food!"

As you can see, this is really a list of story elements and story premises, and almost none of these are fully fleshed out, fully realized stories. It then becomes incumbent upon your team to take these ideas and structure them in a compelling way to create a narrative that will have an emotional impact on the audience.

Step 4—Brand Narrative First Draft. Now, here is a first draft of The Pureffic Signature Origin Story:

"I'm hungry!" It's the winter of 2014. My name is Shalini Chandra and I'm a doctor at Johns Hopkins. But right now, I'm a patient who has just had tongue cancer surgery. During the early months after my surgery, my family and friends gathered around our dining table for delicious meals that I could only see and smell, while I drank my meals from a mug.

It was horrible, but what alternative did I have? I couldn't chew and swallow solid food. So at every chance I got, I would drum up my strength and go foraging through the wilds of supermarket aisles for foods that I could chew and swallow.

Each time I returned with the same bland cups of applesauce or mashed potato buds. I was miserable until a few days later when my life changed, thanks to my kind friend and next-door neighbor. Fellow Johns Hopkins's physician Suchitra Paranji came over with a cup of smooth and thick butternut squash soup.

I loved it so much, I asked her where she found it and could I please have some more. She responded that she created it with all natural ingredients from scratch in her kitchen. This was the birth of Pureffic, and Suchitra and I became the cofounders of Pureffic Gourmet Foods.

As hospital-based physicians, we see patients every day who struggle with chewing and swallowing disorders, many of whom can't cook for themselves. Through our nutritious and delicious gourmet foods, we hope to provide a way to bring everyone back to the dining table. (And please note: For every purchase of a Pureffic Gourmet Food Product, 50 cents will be donated to our dysphagia not-for-profit foundation once it is established.)

Step 5—Revision and Rewriting. All good stories only get to be that way as a result of lots of rewriting. So, I gave the team notes and notes and notes, and they kept reworking the stories until they were well-polished works of art.

Step 6—Testing and Fine-Tuning. We shared the Brand DNA/slogan, logo, and brand narrative with business associates, family, and friends to get feedback. What was working and what wasn't? What led to questions and what was clear?

And then we revised some more.

Step 7—Brand Narrative Fruition Across All Media. Once Pureffic finishes its funding efforts, they will use the capital to create videos and a Website that will spread their message across all digital media forms. They are also considering crowdfunding sources such as Kickstarter and even trying to appear on TV shows such as *Restaurant Startup* and *Shark Tank*. With such a great origin story and such an important purpose, they've got a wonderful chance to be a real success.

||||||||||||||||||||||||||||||||||

Next, I got to speak with storyteller, creative director, and all-around marketing whiz Al Pirozzoli, about brand narratives. This is his take on things:

RK: What role do you see storytelling playing in branding and marketing today?

AP: Storytelling in advertising is often abandoned to the flashy no concept, people dancing, animal spokesmen, and on it goes. I'm not suggesting there isn't any company out there employing stories, but they are far and few between. Storytelling is crucial to successful messaging of the brand's personality. Nothing draws, holds, and creates recall more than stories that actually relate to the consumer. I realize we only have 30 to 60 seconds in a TV spot, and moments in a print ad and Website, so telling a story is now more vital than ever. The best one can do in these formats is convey mini-stories, but that forces the creative director and team to understand the brand like never before. In tough economic times people still buy, but they are much more likely to discriminate.

RK: How do you create, cultivate, and sustain lifelong relationships with customers via digital narratives across all forms of media?

AP: Storytelling is the key to building affinity. With all the research and experiences we have under our belt in advertising, one would think advertisers and their agencies would clearly understand this. Cultivation of customers has always been and will always be centered on developing affinity. If you get lost in the technology of the digital platform and forget the process of building affinity, you will not see long-term loyalty.

To my understanding, a brand narrative (BN) is essentially the history and the future focus of a particular brand. This is crucial because it should, if produced properly, give a brand a real sense of continuity. Further, it offers a way for the consumer to belong to something that has some particular meaning, which equals affinity. Well communicated stories—BNs—that have the ability to transform into new social changes and consumer likes and dislikes are timeless.

Your brand is your story. If that isn't true, you don't have a story; you are promoting a fable that consumers will see through. BNs *are* stories, and do have a beginning, middle, but hopefully no ending. I don't subscribe to the idea that you create a BN. It must already exist and be uncovered and then communicated. Consistency is key. As to control, if you don't control your BN, others will.

Quick cut to Lego. Who doesn't know what that word means? The company has endured for some 80 years or so. Their narrative? Always the same: provide a product that engages young people to think and act out creativity. They stay current by joint ventures with movies, NASA, and many others. No doubt they control the content of their messages, but they never change the essence of the brand's personality.

RK: How do you use stories to *emotionally differentiate* any brand from all of the others in the same category and how has storytelling moved toward brand narratives told by many creators online?

AP: First, I think the common mistake is the way companies attempt to build a BN based on their product's attributes.

Generally speaking, most products offer the same or similar attributes. My wife uses L'Oreal products. Oil of Olay makes very similar claims, and so do others. The BN for L'Oreal creates an emotionally unique connection with its followers: *Because I'm Worth It*. That's not a product attribute; it's a consumer result that no other brand can claim even if they can deliver it.

When you think about it, those four simple words are actually a brand narrative that imprints itself on those who accept and believe it to be true. In terms of social media, smart marketers have tremendous opportunities to engage their consumers in telling their stories. Media technology may change, but the brand narrative, if handled well, doesn't change. The application to its consumers evolves. Bloggers are a tremendous advance to BN. They move mass communications to a personal, one-on-one level. That's powerful because it develops engagement. People seek relationships and through social media have that opportunity, both with other brand evangelists and the brand itself.

RK: Do you have a specific process with which you craft brand narratives that you would be willing to share with readers?

AP: I developed a method called Motivated Abilities Pattern Process (MAPP), which takes the client's brand through an idiosyncratic process. This is typically applied to people, but it works efficiently for discovering and/or supporting a BN reality.

—Al Pirozzoli, Creative Director/Storyteller, Pirozzoli.com

Storytelling Fundamentals and Prof. K.'s Three-Step Narrative Development Process

||||||||||||||||||||||||||||||||||||||||||||||||||||||||||||||||||||||||||||||||||||||||||||||||||||||||||||||||||||||||||||||||||||||||||

Do not despise the story. A lost gold coin is found
by means of a penny candle; the deepest truth
is found by means of a simple story.

—Ancient proverb

Let us now start to break stories down further. What types of business narratives are used on a daily basis with companies small and large? How many of these stories are consciously constructed and what are the fundamental rules behind these narratives? In this chapter, I hope to offer some answers to these and other questions relating to storytelling.

An interactive exercise

I begin most of my seminars with a little interactive exercise. So, now, I'd like to try it here with you. If you will indulge me and be so kind, please lift your hand, point at yourself, and freeze.

Are you pointing at your chest or at your head?

Usually when I'm dealing with a room full of executives, where do you think the majority of their fingers are pointing?

Many psychologists would argue that where you point when you are asked this question shows where your unconscious mind locates your true self.

Are you cerebrally based or emotionally-based? Are you intellectually driven or heart-centered? Do you lead with your head or your heart?

After engaging in this interactive exercise, I then spend the next few minutes trying to convince the room full of intellectually driven writers that to achieve further success, their goal now has to be about lowering their finger to their heart. It has to be about getting in touch with their soul, their authentic, true self. And I argue that the best way to do that is by working on their storytelling skills.

When I push in this direction, initially there always seems to be a certain amount of resistance. I can hear it now: "Yeah, but I'm an executive with a lot at risk. I can't just change the way we do things here overnight."

I understand this resistance. It makes sense, because the skill set that is most rewarded and allows most people to succeed in school is usually not the same skill set that allows people to be good storytellers.

Please indulge me for a while longer, and try to open your heart and soul to becoming a better storyteller. All it takes is a willingness to give it a try as you read on. Trust me: It's worth it. The rewards will go far beyond just telling a good tale or selling a few more bars of soap.

The basic elements of story

What makes for a good story? And how can that be learned and applied to your business?

There's an old Indian proverb that says, "The shortest distance between a human being and the truth is a story." In essence, that is what a good storyteller can and must do: involve his or her audience via a story that carries them all the way to the truth. This involvement is the key to persuasion. Stories can allow you to take seemingly dry material and involve people emotionally in your presentation.

In other words, a good story can actually make your audience care as much about what you are talking about as you do!

In a nutshell, what many writers fail to see is that storytelling is about more than just proving how intelligent, erudite, and well-versed you are. So just breathe and relax. What a relief! Finally, the pressure's off.

In fact, a good storyteller knows that it's his or her job to get out of the way of the story. In other words: *It ain't about you, baby! It's about the story you are telling!*

What you must come to realize is that piling on information might prove that you know a lot of facts or have a lot of technical or scientific knowledge, but it does not necessarily create any sort of emotional connection. And many times, it ends up being this emotional connection that makes your story really sing.

Now, I'd like you to look at your favorite TV commercial, movie, or book, and think about which storytelling elements were used to connect you to the story.

I bet the storyteller had a single protagonist that you could connect with. I also bet that the story had dramatic action that was full of ups and downs and surprises. Beyond that, there were probably credible situations and lots of conflict.

The example I am always drawn to is one of my favorite TV commercials from my younger days. Do you remember the old

Michael J. Fox Diet Pepsi commercial? It follows the Golden Rule to the letter. An engaging character, Michael J. Fox, wants to get a Diet Pepsi to impress his attractive new female neighbor. There are several obstacles keeping him from achieving his goals, but, in the end, he finally succeeds. Along the way, there are ups and downs, dramatic action and surprises, and even comedy to keep you watching and caring.

Even though this short spot was made in 1986, I have never forgotten it and love the way the Diet Pepsi people were able to tell a compelling little story in a short amount of time.

Learning from the best

Where can a person who wants to improve their storytelling look for help?

All the work I've done through the years has shown me that to really learn about storytelling, one needs to go outside the classroom and explore the places where stories are king. Think about it: Who are the people making a living by telling stories, who really understand the art of spinning an engaging and compelling story?

In general, there tend to be clusters of them in Hollywood, in Washington, DC, and on Madison Avenue. In other words, to really understand storytelling, all writers should look at the best mass media, the most eloquent political communications, and the finest commercial advertisements, and ask themselves, "What are these storytellers doing successfully (or unsuccessfully) that I can learn from?"

But wait—I can hear dissenting voices: "I just want to be better at *selling my product* and creating deeper engagement in my company and with our staff, clients, and customers. What do Mad Men or Washington politicos have to teach me?"

This is a valid point, but these worlds are not mutually exclusive. Politicos and advertising execs all know that they have to deliver their messages in an engaging way that allows consumers to accept and retain what they've said. This, then, is the essence of what a good story can do; and it can't be said enough: When properly presented, there is no more compelling means of communication.

Look around the country today and what you will see is that many people believe they can communicate best by information-dumping, usually via PowerPoint. The rules are changing, though, and audiences have a shorter attention span than ever.

Stories as filters and frames

Once we understand and accept the fact that the average person can take in only so much information, especially when that information is complicated and technical, it is fair to assume that much of any presentation, especially a technical one, will *not* be retained nor create a personal connection with your business.

Stories, however, are a comfortable means of communication and enriching connection. As I mentioned earlier, they have the great advantage of being non-hierarchical.

In fact, because most people tend to remember only three bits of information at a time, according to studies on clustering and memory, a story is one of the most effective means to cluster a large amount of information into one packet of knowledge that can be retained. In essence, stories are a good way to summarize and simplify information; they are a good filter and framework for average people to retain large clusters of information.

Actually, it is human nature to assimilate facts, order them, and make connections between those facts until they are assembled together in the form of a story. This is the way we construct our reality; we provide causal connections between discrete facts, and then these connections congeal into a story. In *Stranger Than Fiction*, author Chuck Palahniuk says, "We spend our lives looking for evidence—facts and proof—that support our story."

This aspect of human nature was illustrated in a famous experiment involving pantyhose and women. In the late 1970s, Timothy Wilson and Richard Nisbett, two psychologists, set up an experiment. They had four pairs of pantyhose that were labeled A, B, C, and D. Women were asked to hold, examine, and decide which pair of pantyhose they preferred. As the women went from left to right, they tended to prefer the pair on the right side, D, the most and the pair on the left side, A, the least.

And can you guess what the real truth was behind this whole experiment?

Well, the amazing fact at the core of this experiment was that all four pairs of pantyhose were *identical!*

Yes, we, as human beings, are constantly creating stories. So when asked to give reasons for why they preferred D over all the others, the women all created stories to explain their choices. They talked about things like texture and quality. To justify their choice; they created stories that helped them rationalize the choices they'd made.

Timothy Wilson writes about this quality, which he calls the "adaptive unconscious," in his book *Strangers to Ourselves*. He states, "The causal role of conscious thought has been vastly overrated." We write stories to explain our actions. And this experiment also shows the huge difference between the way we *think* we choose and the ways we *really* choose.

The narrative fallacy

Nassim Nicholas Taleb, in his wonderful book *The Black Swan: The Impact of the Highly Improbable*, talks of the human propensity to create stories as something that leads to a "narrative fallacy." In Taleb's words, "The narrative fallacy is the creation of a story post-hoc so that an event will seem to have a cause."

It reflects our need to fit a story or pattern to a series of connected or disconnected facts. Taleb believes that most people are more comfortable seeing the world as something structured, ordinary, and comprehensible.

Think about this in terms of the story about how your parents first met. Most likely, this story deals with seemingly random events, but these events have been rewritten and/or re-contextualized to have a fated or predestined quality to them. For example, the story might go something like this: "Your father never used to go to that restaurant, but for some reason he chose to go there on that day, and well, the rest is history."

The more we think about it, the clearer it becomes that story-telling is much more than just something that is done around the campfire or with children at bedtime. Maybe the most compelling way to illustrate our brain's *deep-seated need* to create narratives is the fact that we dream.

In our dreams, we aren't thinking up a story, we are creating a story to fit all the memories, which include those being moved from short-term to long-term storage and those that are being thrown in the trash. While our brains are sorting through them all, we need to string all that stuff into something which makes sense and that then becomes our nightly dream narrative. Hence, both during the day and at night while we sleep, we are constantly sorting through the events of our lives to create narratives.

This reminds me of the story of how the tradition of a Christmas tree came to England in Queen Victoria's time. Within 10 or 20 years of this tradition being adopted in England, people were tell-ing stories of how they remember celebrating Christmas and sitting under the tree at their grandparents' house. Suddenly, something brand-spanking new went right back to biblical times. We can't help it. We are always creating narratives, and sometimes they aren't even true.

And it is worth noting that storytelling is an essential form of communication that, as an art form, can be learned and developed. At its heart, much of the storytelling you will be using is about persuasion, about showing others what you want them to know or understand via a narrative. As Bill Bernbach said, "Persuasion happens to be not a science, but an art" (*https://en.wikipedia.org/wiki/William_Bernbach*).

Stories as the rules of the game

Without myths, without religious beliefs, and without stories, life is essentially arbitrary. Things live. Things die. Nature consumes itself and goes on. There is no inherent meaning in natural processes until they are placed within a context, a mythic system, a story.

Once a convincing story has been constructed, *voila*! What was once arbitrary is now endowed with meaning and structure. There is a beginning, a middle, and an end. Stories help cluster the random information of our life together in a way that endows this game of life with meaning.

Stories are the dominant form in which we think and dream. Just keep reminding yourself that your audience is trained to receive stories, and it's up to you to tap into their story receptors. Remember, too, the stories that work the best—the ones that stay with us and affect us most deeply—are the ones that speak to us not only on a rational level but also, and often more importantly, on an emotional level.

Stories must allow us to engage and connect. No matter how rational we consider ourselves to be, the truth is simply this: A majority of all that we do is not driven by rational impulses. We are irrational, unconscious creatures. A great storyteller intuitively knows this. With a good story, a talented storyteller can speak directly to your subconscious and hook you without you ever even understanding how or why.

Let me illustrate this phenomenon by moving into the realm of the supermarket. What stories, you may ask, are at play here? Well, I'd argue that when you walk down the supermarket aisle and stop in the soap section, you have to choose between a multitude of different brands of soap bars that all essentially do the same thing: clean. In the end, the brand you choose will be the one that has told the story that speaks most directly to you.

If you chose Dove, it probably has something to do with the feeling of purity that you associate with this product. If, instead, you reached for Irish Spring, well, you've been drawn in by a different story, one that speaks of a stronger, more "manly" lifestyle as well as to the fresh and natural beauty of Ireland.

Thus, a brand, company, or salesperson that is doing their job well is intuitively telling you the right story, the right way. A good story that is so compelling that you can't help but listen and buy into is one that inevitably leads you to buying into that product as well. In other words, a successful storyteller educates by engagement and not manipulation.

With this understanding, it becomes incredibly valuable to determine what story you are telling and, if it is not working, to learn how to tell a new story that works better. When thinking in terms of stories, it is important to realize that a story is comprised not just of its text.

A story exists within its context and speaks beyond itself through its subtext. Thus, with a deep understanding of the power, meanings, and ramifications of the story's text, context, and subtext, a storyteller can do wonders.

There once were two young fish,
Who were swimming along one day when they
Happened to meet an older fish who said,
"Yo kids, how's the water today?"
The young fish kept swimming until one turned to the other and asked,
"Wait a second, what the hell is water?"

Storytelling is everywhere; we just don't always notice it. Like the water that fish swim in or the air we breathe, it's all around us. A well-constructed and well-told story can be an incredibly powerful instrument with which to create an emotional connection between you and your audience.

So, now, I hope you are really starting to think about the stories you hear every day, the stories you are telling, and maybe even the stories underneath many of the common activities you engage in.

Which of the stories in your life or about your brand or your company do you think are the most effective and why?

Prof. K.'s Three-Step Narrative Development Process:

Step 1—A single sentence/logline

Before you start creating your story, can you articulate the general premise in a single sentence? And does the premise really floor people when you tell it to them? Until everyone says, *"Wow!* That's an awesome idea!" please do not go forward.

Let me explain why I believe this. First of all, having this kind of clarity really helps create a coherent, compelling tale. And, secondly, if the story is something that you want people to talk about (online or offline) or even tweet about, then they are going to do so with a sentence or two. That's all they will have time for and that's all that is necessary. And if it is really engaging, people will be hooked and your story will spread. So this is the concept behind this single-sentence descriptor.

You need not tell your whole story in one sentence. But do try to at least capture the general idea and the premise so it titillates others to want to learn about the whole story.

Step 2—The big seven questions!

When push comes to shove, in my mind there really are just seven essential questions that all storytellers must ask themselves. No matter what kind of story they are working on or what genre. These seven questions remain the same.

So here they are, and I hope that you are intuitively already asking yourself these questions as you create new narratives. If not, try them. Also, feel free to take a story you've already written and run it through these seven questions to really learn about the true nature of your narrative.

1. Who is your main character? (You can only have one.)
2. What does your main character want/need/desire? (In other words, what is their dramatic problem? This dramatic problem needs to be articulated in terms of both an inner emotional need and a concrete, physical need that exists outside the protagonist.)
3. Who/what keeps him/her from achieving what he/she wants? (Who/what are the apparent and true antagonists standing in the way?)

4. How in the end does he/she achieve what he/she wants in an unexpected, interesting, and unusual way? (For example, even in a love story when we know the lovers are going to get together, we must not know how they are going to get together.)

5. What are you trying to say by ending the story this way? (What are your *themes* and motifs?)

6. How do you want to tell your story? (Who should tell it, if anyone, and what narrative devices should you employ?)

7. How do your main character and any supporting characters *change* through the course of the story? (This is all about character arc; it is this change that makes the story emotionally compelling to your audience.)

Step 3—The step outline

Now, if you've succeeded in answering all the big seven questions, you should have good clarity as to what your story is really about. *Great!* Then it's time to take that story further and really put it through the wringer to see if it really has what it takes to work! (And if not, don't fret; soon, I'll provide some other valuable tricks to help you make it work.)

Now let's try to put the story back together in the form of a step outline—also called a scene or beat outline. Call it what you will, but it's just basically a series of sentences or small paragraphs outlining the story as a whole. At this point, don't get caught up in great lines of dialogue or wonderful turns of phrases (of course, if you do think of one, write it down immediately before you forget it). But for now, dialogue is not your main concern. What you want to do here is get the gist of your story out in the open so you can see what you have, what's working, and where you have major problems.

Note that you can do this process with both a story that's already been written and/or with an idea that has yet to be fleshed out. If you've got an old story you want to rework, try to do a step outline where you articulate in a sentence or two the purpose of every big moment in the story. If you have just an idea, imagine what each beat or event in the story should do in telling your story as a whole, and record those in the order that you think they'll take place.

Either way, seeing all the major moments in your story laid out in front of you should be really illuminating. If in doing this, you soon realize that there are major gaps in your story, then this process has forced you to see where there are holes and now all you have to do is figure out how to fill them with the necessary story elements. Easy as pie, right?

I like doing this as a Word file on my computer, because once I get all the major scenes or moments laid out properly and in order in my outline, then all I need to do is describe the settings and actions, add dialogue, and—*voila!*—instant first draft of my story.

Case study: Pond's Flawless White

Let me now show you a bit more about how stories work by giving you a case study of an experience I had working on an international brand. (Note: I have worked with many brands and companies, but in many of those cases I have signed confidentiality agreements, so I am unable to share those stories. However, in this case, I worked with the Pond's Flawless White team on that product, and the global brand director has given me the okay to tell our tale. So here goes.)

The Pond's Flawless Skin Care team had a problem. They had a great new product that studies showed could radically improve women's skin in only seven days. So, then, you might ask, what was the problem?

Well, how do you convey this information in a convincing and credible way to the target market? The global brand director did not believe this could happen with an image of some skin molecules and before-and-after shots of a model with damaged and then improved skin.

He knew a compelling story would be the most persuasive way to do this. And he was eager to try something new. He also knew that engagement was way down with TV viewers, as more and more of them spent their time watching TiVo and shows on the Internet. In other words, people were trying different ways to avoid watching commercials, and if this one was going to work, it had to be special and really draw people in.

He and I discussed the idea of telling his Pond's Flawless Skin story in a serial/soap-opera-style narrative that would extend over several TV commercials. This was a huge risk because the shooting costs would be exorbitant and there was also a chance of confusing or alienating viewers.

However, the upside was even more monumental. I loved the idea and knew that if we could hook viewers in the first commercial, we'd have them yearning to watch the rest. Then, instead of clicking away from the commercials, they'd be going online in search of our commercials and even e-mailing them to friends and family.

We had our core concept, and we knew the risks and returns involved. But we weren't nervous because we knew what this challenge necessitated: a story so gripping that viewers would tune in again and again. We also knew that, because the product showed dramatic results through seven days, our drama must also take place through the course of seven days.

The global brand director, a talented team of copywriters, and I set to work. We brainstormed stories. I gave notes. We engaged in the three-step storytelling development process. We found our protagonist, our obstacles, and our surprising ending. We made sure that it was thematically consistent with the brand. We kept in mind that our hero had to change for the good through the course of the story.

There were outlines and more notes. And then draft after draft and more notes. Finally, they shot it. And we had ourselves a series of short films that we thought told an emotionally powerful story and also conveyed the product benefits we needed the audience to know.

But the big question remained: Would people really care enough about the characters and the story in our ads to want to watch them all? (Well, if you are curious, feel free to go to YouTube and watch the Pond's Flawless White "7 Days to Love" TV commercial and see for yourself.) I'm proud to say that the story tested through the roof, and more importantly, it was a huge hit. Women loved it! Product sales soared! And we were thrilled.

The fun wasn't over yet, though. Because things went so well with that brand, the good people at Pond's decided to roll out a bit more prestigious product, Pond's Gold Radiance. In that case, they needed an even more effective advertising campaign because the product was going to be more expensive than the other Pond's products.

This called for the big story guns. The global brand director flew all of the marketing execs, creatives, and me to Bali for a week to bang our heads together and come up with something extraordinary. Here is the sequence of events that happened during our weeklong sojourn on that magical island:

First, the strategy planner came to us with the brief, which emphasized the core concept of eternal love. It was clear to him, based on the consumer research, that the women who were the target demographic for this product feared losing the love of their husbands due to looking older. They wanted a silver bullet to keep looking youthful (who doesn't?) and to ensure their husbands' eternal love.

So I gave a series of lectures on romantic storytelling, and then we did a series of writing exercises. We came up with a winning image: a gold wedding band. We also came up with a winning drama: a love story that takes place through the centuries between two star-crossed lovers who are torn apart and finally reunite in the present day.

But that was just the beginning. The script needed lots of work, so the copywriters did draft after draft, and the global brand director and I gave notes. Within months, we had a final script that told a compelling story and also featured the radiant gold ring and the product.

The results were phenomenal! And the TV commercial won several awards. (Go to YouTube and check out Pond's Gold Radiance "Eternal Love" TV commercial.) The question that now inevitably arises is this: What if you *don't* have millions of dollars to do big TV commercials and take your whole team to Bali?

The answer is simply, well, just hire me. And you and I can go to Bali and we can leave the rest of the team at home and then do a low-budget production. In all seriousness, the answer is really quite simple. Big budgets make it easier to do fancy campaigns with lots of slick TV commercials, but in the end these days, one can tell stories in print or through the Internet for very little money and still make a huge impact.

The key factor is not one of budget. It is about understanding your product, your audience, and your needs with what's happening next with your brand, and then creating a new brand narrative that emotionally engages your core target market.

That is all, and that is more than enough.

CHAPTER 8

Prof. K.'s Storytelling Rules and Tools, Part 1— Structure, Structure, Structure

〡〡〡

If history were taught in the form of stories,
it would never be forgotten.
—Rudyard Kipling, *The Collected Works*

When a story isn't working, usually it's a function of structural issues. Hence, let's dive deeper now and enter the world of structure. As we've already covered three-act structure and my three-step story development process, what we'll cover now are further concepts and principles that will allow anyone to make their stories more effective.

When we talk about structure, what we are referencing is the ordering and pacing of the story elements. In other words, which scenes and actions do you need to put in, which do you need to leave out, and in what sequence? To explain this further, let me quote a Hollywood icon. Legend has it that the great film director Billy Wilder, once said that if you have a problem with the ending of your story, then don't change the ending—revise act one. What this calls attention to is the rule of structure—setting up and paying off. This illustrates the need for every good storyteller to implement the right structural changes so that a story which lacks power suddenly comes to life and works. Here are some easy-to-follow and entertaining rules and tools that anyone can implement:

Be a scene stealer

The quality and order of your scenes, your story moments, your Lego-blocks of narrative, if you will, determine whether your story will really work or not. So, let us not move forward without spending a moment to look at what makes a great scene. In a nutshell, there are no hard and fast rules, but in terms of scene construction, these are my favorites:

1. Get in the scene late and get out of the scene early!
2. Each scene needs its own good raison d'être.
3. Scenes are ruled by causality. (So, every scene is necessary and forces the story forward.)

Simply put, if you choose the right combination of scenes, juxtaposed together in the right order, never losing sight that each scene must push the story forward while combining the main plot elements with sub-plot elements, you can create a truly compelling story. But if you break the story down into a scene/moment outline, you can really see what it is, what is working, and what needs to be fixed.

All the scenes that are included should be essential to furthering the story. Each should have a raison d'être, and there should be some change in the story's status quo by the end of every scene.

As you journey from scene to scene, think of alternating between zeniths and nadirs, high and low moments, happy and sad, interiors and exteriors, so that, like a great symphony, there is a rhythm and musicality to your story.

The snapshot solution

Now, let's look at the scene itself. If it is feeling flat, think in terms of snapshots. Imagine the scene as a Polaroid. What specific objects in the image would be most telling? You obviously can't describe it all, so what specifics elements can you describe to bring it all to life? Think viscerally in terms of textures, colors, and the other senses beyond the visual. For instance, I know snapshots don't have smells, but what smells might add to really bringing the scene to life? Smell is a powerful sense that is often overlooked.

With this deep understanding of the basic chapters/scenes/moments in your story, you should now be on comfortable ground in developing your story. The rest should be fun. You know what scenes you need. You know where the scenes begin and end. All you have to do now is flesh them out.

Listen to the characters' voices as they talk to each other. Capture the smells and important visual aspects of each moment. If you have a good outline, facing the blank page is not overwhelming because you will not face writer's block. You know exactly what every scene needs to do when you begin to caress the keyboard. You know where the story is going and it's up to you to bring each scene to life!

The world's slowest tailor

A young man went to a tailor shop to get a beautiful custom-made tuxedo for his wedding. The old tailor measured the young man, wrote up the order, and took a deposit. Then the young man said, "I'm getting married in a month, so I need it pretty soon!"

"Well, that's gonna be tricky. It's going to take me a while to do it right."

"I really need it in three weeks or less."

"Oh. Okay," the tailor said. "Don't worry. I'll make sure it's ready on time."

Reluctantly, the young man left. Worried the old tailor wouldn't have his tuxedo finished in time, he called the tailor's shop once a day to check on the progress. Every day, the tailor assured him that his tuxedo would be ready in time.

A week went by, then two weeks, then three weeks, and every time he called, the young man got the same reply. "It's not ready yet."

Finally, on the day before the wedding, the old tailor told the young man to come by to pick it up.

The young man ran over to the shop and, sure enough, his tuxedo was done and it was perfect. He paid the tailor, took his tuxedo, and started to leave, but then stopped at the door. He turned to look at the old tailor and said, "Sir, I have to say this: With all due respect, it took God only seven days to make the whole world, and it took you 31 days to make just one tuxedo."

The old tailor answered, "Well, look at the world and look at this tuxedo!"

⁕

What is the meaning of this story as it relates to narratives?

Well, I think it's the perfect story for writers to hear and think about. Like the slow tailor, we writers are seeking perfection in a non-perfect world. It's a long, hard struggle, but one worth doing. There is so little we can control in the world around us, so we actually must hold tightly and be very careful with the words we create, the sentences we craft, and the stories we share with others.

We can't control whether the type of story we are writing is hot or cold in the industry. We can't control whether people want big-budget or low-budget projects, but we can control our story.

Our story is the only thing we *can* control and we must not let it out into the world too soon. One of the biggest mistakes writers make is simply this: They release their work out into the world too soon.

When we are working on a project, we tend to get excited about it and are unable to see if it's truly finished and ready to be shown to others. So most of us tend to think we are done long before a project should truly be let out into the world.

The key is to hold on and revise. To aid you as you move forward, here are a slew of rules, tools, and methods to help you as you spend hours rewriting and perfecting your art. These are the result of 25 years spent writing and rewriting both my own work and the work of others. They are not in any particular order, but just a smattering of concepts that hopefully will prove to be helpful to you.

Because storytelling can be taught, these rules and tools are more than just fun little lessons; they are essential guidelines for you to implement in order to master the construction of compelling narratives.

The 2 a.m. syndrome

This first one relates to the phenomenon that I just mentioned.

When I am working with someone on their story, I always urge them to slow down and put their document away for a while. Revisit it only when you can read it objectively and with distance. Most of us suffer from what I call the "2 a.m. syndrome." In other words, many times when we finish writing something around 2 a.m., we will be convinced it is brilliant. But when we wake up the next day and read it, we discover that it is really full of flaws.

It is hard to be objective, truly objective, with one's own work. This is why I spend a lot of time consulting with others. The truth is that it is usually only others who can see what needs to be done to one's story to really make it shine. And, of course, this is why every publishing house has editors.

So I urge the people I am working with to put their stories away for a while. Then, when they are ready to revisit them, I suggest they try taking their story through the following checklist of interesting rules and tools. Note, though, this checklist is really just a whole bunch of different criteria that I have collected through the years. Some of it might seem more useful than other parts. That's okay. The key is to find what works for you. And some of the questions that I want you to ask yourself as you go through this chapter might seem self-evident to you.

Well, that's good, too. That means that you are already doing a lot of the right things necessary to tell a great story. The main thing is that by going through this process you can weed out the story problems and further develop your story, so once you send it out to the world, it is really sound.

The storyteller and audience's contract

In the end, with good storytelling, there is a contract. The storyteller says, "I am going to tell you a good story," and the audience says, "I am going to believe you, connect with you, and suspend my disbelief, but I am only one false line of dialogue or unmotivated action away from re-establishing my disbelief and, instantly, disconnecting from you."

I am always thinking that this is a possibility. I can lose my audience with one false move. So I am always questioning: Does this story satisfy me intellectually, emotionally, viscerally? Does it move me? Touch me? Where? How?

Tell good stories and always keep revising the weak points in your story so that the audience stays completely immersed in your story world.

The Evelyn Krevolin credo of credibility

Storytelling is about creating an immersive world for your audience, and as I just pointed out, your audience is always one step away from removing themselves from this storytelling-induced trance state. So, you are in trouble the moment the audience thinks, "Hey! Wait a second. C'mon now, this couldn't happen" or "Wait a second. This feels wrong!"

This credo became clear to me when I used to watch movies with my mother, Evelyn Krevolin. Whenever we'd be sitting in a movie theatre or at home in front of the television, and a hole in the story appeared, she would always slap me on the shoulder and say,

"Richie, you're a storytelling expert. What's going on here? This makes no sense, right? Right?"

And you know what? She was always correct. Even though she wasn't a writer, she intuitively sensed a problem in the story. She was initially immersed in the story and then something knocked her out of the story world and, as a result, she reached out to me for an explanation.

In essence, she had initially suspended her disbelief and then, when the storytelling got lazy or took a misstep, she sensed this and was no longer able to suspend her disbelief. Your job as a storyteller is to make sure that this never happens and to construct a consistent, credible world.

The two-by-four wooden plank principle

This phenomenon of people pulling away from a story when they feel like they are being lectured to is an example of what I like to call the two-by-four principle. In other words, nobody likes to feel like they're being hit on the head with a wooden plank. Your job is to enchant the heart of your audience, whoever that audience may be.

You've got to get in under the radar, drop your bomb, and get out. You do that by entertaining people, by enchanting their hearts. The word "recognition" comes from the Latin word for "knowledge," and so when we "recognize," we see something we already know in the story. A good storyteller always taps into recognized territory, but he or she does it via a new story, a fresh set of characters or circumstances.

Finally, it's worth noting that everything I'm talking about here relies upon a consciousness of audience response. Therefore, no matter how good a storyteller you are, there is a need to test and tweak any story you tell. That's why Hollywood uses test screenings before they release a film, Broadway's theatrical producers do a series of previews, and many lawyers test their openings and closings by engaging in mock trials with potential jurors in the locale of their upcoming trial. All of these are done to discover how the story being told is affecting the emotional response of the audience.

In the end, it's about them, not you. It's about the audience, not the storyteller.

And let me be clear: The key thing here is *legitimate* subtle manipulation. Whether you like it or not, as a storyteller you must be slightly *manipulative!* It is your job to alter (that is, manipulate) the story in order to create the emotional response you desire. Therefore, please note that I am not referencing manipulation in the negative sense of the word. Nobody likes being manipulated or a person who is a manipulator.

In the end, all storytelling is about manipulation and what differentiates good storytelling from bad is the legitimacy of that manipulation. Did the storyteller move me so I wanted to applaud at the end of the story, or did he/she anger and frustrate me so that I did feel manipulated and, as a result, I wanted to reject the story? A good manipulator knows that those who they are manipulating must never feel manipulated; instead, they need to feel as if they've just willingly gone along on a great ride!

Why should the audience care?

The audience cares because they have connected with your characters and story. And to keep them caring, you need to maintain the suspense and tension. The two biggest notes I usually give my clients are "Who cares?" and "Need more tension!"

Your audience needs to care, and they care when there is good tension that keeps them engaged. It is tension that keeps them involved in the story. It is tension that keeps them wanting to know more. And if there is concern for the character, and big stakes, and a fear of failure, and tons of uncertainty, there will be *tension*.

Yes, all of these factors are necessary, and when combined together, they equal tension and good storytelling.

The Wicked Witch of the West syndrome

Many times stories start out great, but soon sputter. If you are having trouble keeping your story going, look at what was done in *The*

Wizard of Oz. At first, Dorothy wanted to run away from home, and then once she got to Oz she wanted to find the Wizard, and then once she found him, in order to get back home, she had to get the Wicked Witch's broomstick. Her search for this broomstick drove the rest of the story forward.

So, I always ask my students, what is your broomstick engine? What is it that your main character wants that will drive the story forward? And this *want* must always be clearly articulated in the story for the audience to care, even if it changes through the course of the story, as it does in *The Wizard of Oz*.

The never-ending subway train at night law

It is an incredibly difficult thing to maintain a coherent and themat-ically unified story through 100 pages or, for that matter, through 10 pages. Thus, if your story feels episodic, or if you are told it is episodic, sorry, but your story is in trouble. The best metaphor I ever heard for an episodic story is that it feels like "a never-ending subway train at night."

So then, how can you insure that your story does not suffer this episodic fate? Well, in an episodic story, the scenes might work on their own, but not together as a whole. Therefore, look at your story. Does each scene raise further questions in the reader's mind so that they needs to keep reading the next scenes? Are there questions in each scene, which, when they are answered, will inspire further new questions? And are there some larger, overriding questions and story issues that are only answered at the end of the story?

By confronting these questions, you should be well on your way to making your story episodic-proof.

The aide-memoire technique

Here's a technique I learned in a creative writing class that is very powerful. It is called aide-memoire. This is a process whereby you engage the readers as participants, not merely as spectators. In essence, what you try to do with this technique is strip down your writing so that you don't ever label any emotions. You merely tell the reader what happens; what things taste, smell, look, or sound like, but not what they mean.

Let me give you an example. Take a look at this sentence: "Frank was stressed out and nervous."

Grammatically it's sound, but it tells the reader about Frank's emotional state without letting the reader determine what that emotional state is.

Now, look at this sentence: "Frank wrapped and unwrapped the telephone cord around his ring finger."

This sentence conveys the same information as the previous sentence, but the reader has to visualize Frank's actions and then, as a result of using their imagination, the reader can, on their own, determine that Frank is stressed out and nervous.

In the process, they are drawn into the story, instead of kept at a distance from it. So this technique can help pull readers into the narrative, instead of pushing them away.

The four simplest writing rules ever

Try these on for size! Here are four simple rules that are guaranteed to make your writing, and thus your story, better.

1. Minimize adjectives.
2. Minimize adverbs.
3. Maximize strong action verbs.
4. Place your subject and verb as close together as possible.

CHAPTER 9

Prof. K.'s Storytelling Rules and Tools, Part 2— Character and Dialogue

|||||||||||||||||||||||||||||||||||||||||||||||||||||||||||||||||||||||||||||||||||||||||||||||||||||||||||||||||||||||||||||||||||||||||||

I will tell you something about stories.... They aren't just entertainment. Don't be fooled. They are all we have, you see, all we have to fight off illness and death.
—Leslie Marmon Silko, *Ceremony*

All of these rules and tools are about audience engagement. They are about creating a feeling of relationship with your consumers and/or customers, making them care so they want to stay connected to your brand. This is the goal of most narratives: to create a deep emotional involvement with your story. This chapter will continue with a series of helpful rules and tools related to character and dialogue.

The Lee Van Cleef axiom

One of the most famous bad guys in the history of Western films is Lee Van Cleef. At the end of his life, legend has it that he was asked, "What was it like, spending your life playing bad guys?"

And he responded, "Heck, I've never played a bad guy in my life!"

What I think he was trying to say in this quote is simply that, as an actor, he never thought of himself as a good guy or a bad guy, but merely a human being trying to achieve a goal. If that goal involved killing other people, so be it. He did not bring morality into it, but merely thought in terms of character motivation.

This is a good lesson for writing strong antagonists. Most bad guys don't think of themselves as bad guys. With this in mind, it might be easier to create fully realized antagonists, or at least bad guys, who have no compunction about doing bad things.

The killer and his cute cats syndrome

Every story needs conflict, and that usually comes in the form of an antagonist. Along these lines, the question of humanizing the bad guy always pops up. If a bad guy is just pure evil, he might play like a caricature and hurt your story. But if a bad guy or girl is too compelling and sympathetic, then they could subvert your story. So, how does one create a credible antagonist that helps your story?

The simplest way to humanize a bad guy/gal without making him or her too sympathetic is to give him or her a bevy of cute cats. Of course, you can't just pop in a few kittens and—*voila!*—have a lovable antagonist. What I am saying here is that bad guys have lives, too.

They need to eat and sleep, and they might have pets they love, such as cats. Think about them as fully three-dimensional human beings and then they will play as real in your story, instead of just as caricatures.

The reverse side of this is that if you make them too likable, too three dimensional, and too much of an animal lover, you risk having your audience feel more for them than for your hero. So be careful.

The answer is simply this: Make your antagonist credible, but don't let them overshadow your protagonist.

The V8 edict of endings

Do you remember those old V8 TV commercials when people would forget that they could have had a V8 cocktail and they would smash themselves in the head? I used to love them, and whenever I forgot something I would mimic the V8 head strike.

I bring this up in relation to how things sometimes work at the end of poorly executed stories. A character is at the end of their ropes and then, just when they need some vital bit of information, they think of it and they smash themselves in the head, uttering, "Why didn't I think of this before?"

Most of the time, this device feels just cheap and false. The key to making this kind of thing work is planting and paying off. If the unknown information is planted several times in the story in a subtle way during act one and two, when the character comes to remember it in act three, it will feel organic to the story and not contrived. And, thus, the audience will accept instead of reject it. (See *The Evelyn Krevolin Credo!*)

The coughing blood narrative nuance

In keeping with the V8 concept, there is the character coughing blood syndrome. In a story, if we see a character coughing up blood onto a hanky two or three times during the course of the narrative, we kind of know that they are going to die before the end of the story.

It's not really even a conscious thing, but we feel it.

In real life, when someone coughs blood, it's not a good thing, but they aren't necessarily going to die within the next few hours. This calls attention to a specific fact about storytelling. In well-written stories, all the elements that are in the story are there for a reason, especially any element that is repeated two or three times.

Think about it. The majority of the character's life happens outside of the story and those events that are chosen by the writer to happen in the story are usually there for a specific reason.

Thus, we as the audience start to intuitively pay close attention to that which is given to us in the story. If someone says or does something, be advised that it will probably reappear later and have meaning.

So it is incumbent upon you to plant information in a subtle way that will push your story forward and allow for the events at the end of the story to unfold in a way that all the story elements coalesce by the end.

The puppy on the side of the road principle

As Malcolm Gladwell pointed out in his book *Blink*, first impressions are incredibly important. And the same holds true for all of your stories. It is hugely significant to think about the first time your reader or your audience will meet any of your important characters.

First, consider the setting and moment attached to this first meeting. In romantic comedies, people talk about having a cute meet. However, for any type of story, our initial impression is a big deal and must be something you as the author thinks a lot about.

Where does the scene occur when the audience first meets the protagonist? What do you want to convey by having the scene set here? And what does the protagonist do in his or her first scene to help define him or herself for the audience?

While you are considering this, think about how we can convey lots of information visually and simply. This takes us to the "puppy on the side of the road principle." What I want you to think about with this concept is this: When we first meet your main character, if he or she is walking down the street and past a cute little puppy, how do they respond to the puppy?

This will tell your audience everything they need to know about this character. Do they kick the puppy, feed the puppy, or ignore the puppy? Each choice is a huge indicator of character and we yearn to quickly know what kind of people we are dealing with in your story.

So think about how you first present your characters and what actions you can have them perform.

The Missouri mandate

A good business presentation can get the client to sign on the dotted line and mean millions of dollars in business. A good lawyer can tell a story, create a message that "changes people's behavior," and maybe even get the jury to start thinking about his or her client differently. A good screenwriter can write a script that gets you to see the world differently after reading it. A great playwright can write a play that will change you after only two hours in the theater. And a great novelist—well, of course they can change the world. It's happened before and will happen again.

In all these different mediums, this is usually done by following the cardinal rule of storytelling. As they say in the great "Show Me State" of Missouri (yes, you may have heard it before and you've heard it because it's so important): *Show me; don't tell me!*

This rule is best exemplified by a Chekhov quote about writing in which he says, "Don't tell me the moon is shining. Show me the glint of moonlight on broken glass." This is intuitively what a great storyteller does. He or she shows you the glint and you get the rest.

In other words, it is about leading the audience to water the right way so that they do drink. If your readers think they are coming to their own conclusion by putting together the useful information that you have already given them, then they will feel as if your story allowed them to reach their own opinions and thank you for guiding them to it.

Here's an analogy that might help explain this concept. In essence, as a good storyteller, you need to start thinking like a good math teacher who does not give his or her students the answer to a tough math problem, but gives them the theorem to solve the problem and they come to the right answer on their own.

Perfecting your protagonist

Your hero or protagonist is hugely important to your story. So let's talk about your hero for a minute. There are really two types of heroes: the imperfect hero and the perfect hero. And the imperfect hero is way more interesting. So, I always urge my students to try to create an imperfect hero as their protagonist. This allows the hero to grow, learn, and change during the course of the story. And that makes for good storytelling.

In terms of heroes, think of their special skills versus their special weaknesses. And then through the course of the story, have them get in touch with their strengths to overcome their weaknesses. This should lead to character growth or what I like to call character arc. Your character should never be the same person at the beginning of the story as they are at the end of the story.

The Three Ps property

If your character feels flat or stereotypical, then try to think of them in terms of how to "three-dimensionalize" them. In other words, try to employ what I like to call the "Three Ps" of every person's life:

Professional.

Personal.

Psychological.

You need to know about all aspects of your character's life. For example: What do they do for a living? Where do they work? How much money do they make? What is their personal life like, including family, friends, and home life? And what is their inner or psychological life like?

A character only becomes truly three dimensional when you've considered all three of these aspects for them, and your story only becomes truly three dimensional when you've considered all three of these aspects for all of your characters.

How to have S.U.C.C.E.S.S.

A good story should be many things at once and serve several purposes. I like to think of a good story in terms of an acronym: S.U.C.C.E.S.S. In other words, a good story should be:

Simple.

Unexpected.

Concrete.

Credible.

Emotional.

Succinct.

Spelled properly.

The S.U.C.C.E.S.S. acronym is a helpful checklist as you construct your story. In addition, in Frank Luntz's book, *Words That Work: It's Not What You Say, It's What People Hear,* he provides a similar 10-point checklist that will help ensure that any message will work. His 10 points include, "Simplicity, Brevity, Credibility, Consistency, Novelty, Sound, Aspiration, Visualization, Questioning, and Context."

So whether you like my acronym or Luntz's top 10 qualities, the end result is the same: Both allow you to evaluate a story in order to ensure that it is effective.

Another important point to keep in mind is that your story is something that should be told, not defined. You are merely the guide who ensures that your audience gets taken where they need to be. It is your job to let your audience get the moral of the story from the cumulative impact of the events that you string together.

My mommy needs an operation mandate

In old movies, inevitably the bad guy would reveal that he/she became a gangster because, well, their sweet old mother needed an expensive operation and, frankly, robbing a bank was the only way to get the money because they came from a pre-Obamacare world, were poor, and were underprivileged.

So, what can we take away from this?

First, this feels outdated now, so try not to use it. Second, and more importantly, what it does show is the need to justify a character's action, especially if it is an unethical or illegal one. For us to feel for and understand why a character does what he/she does, there needs to be a good justification that we, as the audience, can relate to.

Unless you want your bad guy to be such an amoral, anti-social psychopath that he just kills for pleasure, you will need to consider the motivations and origins of how someone becomes a "bad guy."

The hostess with the mostess model

Let's say I was new in town and I came to your house for a party and you were busy the whole time in your kitchen preparing food. If you didn't greet me at the door when I arrived, and didn't talk to me while I was there, how do you think I would feel about your party? I'd probably not have very positive things to say about it.

But what if you greeted me at the door with a warm hug and then, one by one, you introduced me to everybody at the party, always bringing up specific things that I share with each partygoer, so that I was quickly able to connect with each and every person there?

That night, when I returned home, how do you think I would feel about this party?

And now, how does this relate to what you're doing in terms of storytelling? In essence, I believe this is a perfect metaphor for what good writers must do. You are the hostess of the party known as your story.

When you are telling your story, you are taking your audience in, connecting them to the characters, and taking them through the world of your story. In fact, you are the hostess (or host) with the mostess.

Way too often, I read a story in which the author introduces several characters on page one and then things get worse from there. It's overwhelming and off-putting. Even if you know your characters and world well, you can't just throw the reader in too quickly. First, you need to have the reader connect with your protagonist and then, and only then, you can take the reader along with the protagonist into the world and have them meet other characters. Additionally, you have to give the right anecdotes at the right time in the right way and in the right order for your audience to get the full picture.

Through your story, you have created a bond of trust, a relationship based upon an honest exchange that has just occurred between you and your audience.

Once this relationship is clear, once you've established trust and engagement between the main character and your audience, and you've then used that bond to enter the world of your story, it's time to think about the dialogue that the characters use within the story. So here are some good rules to follow when engaging in the construction of how people talk.

Less is more dialogue

The key to dialogue is brevity. Many times when we are telling stories in business situations, we can jazz up our stories by adding a little dialogue. Sure, if you can do accents well, add a little accent, but in general I advise my clients to play it safe and be careful of overdoing accents. With that said, dialogue does bring your story to life and it's worth adding when you can.

Maybe my favorite line of dialogue of all time is in the movie *Escape From Alcatraz*, in which Clint Eastwood's character is asked, "What was your childhood like?" and he answers, "Short."

In one word, we've been told all we need to know. Use dialogue when you can to make your story come to life, but use it sparingly.

The artifice of dialogue dictate

A story usually gets its flavor from good dialogue. But what exactly is good dialogue?

The truth is that real life dialogue and good storytelling dialogue are two separate things. Real life dialogue when put in a story does not, in fact, sound real. Instead, it sounds false.

In real life, we may say what we want, but good dialogue in a story is usually not so direct. Sure, there are times in a story when a character must yell, "WATCH OUT FOR THAT SPEEDING MERCEDES COMING STRAIGHT AT YOU!"

But in general, the dialogue that we like best is filled with texture, flavor, and great turns of phrases. It furthers the story, but it does not do it in a straight line. And, ideally, it is more clever and interesting than real-life dialogue.

The Elmer J. Fudd law

As a child, I loved watching the old Bugs Bunny cartoons. I distinctly remember an episode in which Elmer J. Fudd proclaimed something along the lines of, "My name is Elmer J. Fudd, millionaire. I own a mansion and a yacht."

I think I remember this line decades later because it was so, well, incongruous. Even at a tender young age, I knew that human beings don't just declare who and what they are and what they own. And if they did, it was not a very nice thing to do. My mother taught me the virtue of humility, and declaring one's financial status upon meeting someone was just not done and not at all authentic.

So how does this apply to us? Well, way too often, my students have submitted to me work that uses dialogue to convey information that is just too "in your face." Find interesting and visual ways to convey that someone is a millionaire, instead of having them declare their economic status. On video, this is easy. Having them ride up to a meeting in a limousine or Rolls Royce will pretty much do it. In a nutshell, don't use dialogue to convey information that you can do so in a more subtle way.

The artifice (not artificial) ingredient

Artifice is our next key element. Let me explain. If you were to leave a digital audio recorder in a booth in a Burger King where two people were talking, and then transcribe the dialogue verbatim onto a page, it would not read like real dialogue even though, of course, it is a real, verbatim transcription.

You see, one must focus on the appearance of reality or what is called "writing with verisimilitude." Your job as a storyteller is not to create dialogue that is real; your job is to create dialogue that sounds as though it is real and, hopefully, a bit more clever than average interactions. The distinction here—the "sounds as though it is real" part of the equation—is everything.

In the end, most business stories are not going to be that long, so the amount of dialogue should be limited. Within those limits, though, it's always good to pepper your story with a bit of dialogue here and there to help it come alive.

CHAPTER 10

Prof. K.'s Storytelling Rules and Tools, Part 3— The Fine Art of Revision

Art is never finished, it is merely abandoned.
—Oscar Wilde

As Oscar Wilde said, it is true that we must eventually aban-don our stories after reworking them over and over again. Yet, before you give up on rewriting, there are many rules and tools that will help you get your story to the most highly polished, well-crafted version possible. It is only then that your story is ready to be abandoned and released to the world.

The you can always be meaner prerogative

Most of the people whom I do story consulting with are nice. They are good, kind-hearted people who want to be better storytellers.

And that is, many times, their biggest problem. As people, they are just *too nice* to be good storytellers.

Good storytellers must be ruthless, at least when it comes to their characters and the things that happen to them. In fact, as someone who constructs stories, it is your job to figure out the worst, most horrible things that could possibly happen to your characters and then make those very things happen!

Maybe the biggest note that I give is simply, "THAT'S TOO EASY! Things can't happen too easily in your story. There needs to be more conflict!" Often, we make things too simple for our characters and we need to go back and provide more conflict and complications.

This is especially hard for writers who fall in love with their characters. But, alas, how will your characters ever grow if things are easy for them to achieve? In many cases, growth only comes out of adversity, and so it becomes incumbent upon you, as a storyteller, to make the lives of your characters very difficult, and as a result, very dramatic.

Along these same lines, always make your antagonist into a worthy opponent. For it is your antagonist who helps drive the story by constantly putting roadblocks in the way of your protagonist's goals.

The three potential audience positions

There are three potential positions for your audience to be in during a story. They can be equal to, inferior to, or superior to your protagonist at any time in the story. Think about the ramifications of each of these positions and employ them accordingly.

For instance, if you want to create greater tension, you might put your audience in a superior position to your main character. The audience might see a man with a knife hide in the closet. Then, when the main character walks into the room and reaches into the closet, what reaction do you think your audience is going to have?

When your audience is equal to your main character, they know as much as, but no more or less than, the protagonist. This might work in some cases and is worth considering.

In other cases, you might want to have the audience know less than the main character. This happens often in detective stories. The detective has already figured out the case and the audience keeps reading to determine what the characters are doing and why. Hence, by putting the audience in an inferior position, the storyteller has helped insure that the reader will keep turning the page.

What position should your audience be in for your story in order to maximize the potential impact of your narrative?

The North Star theme meme

The North Star remains constant while everything else in the sky revolves around it.

In terms of your story, you should think of the theme as your "North Star." It is your theme that remains constant throughout your narrative. It is your theme that provides the meaning, the moral content to your story.

What is the theme in your story? Is it clear by the end and does your audience understand it by the time the story is over?

Themes are hugely important and are essentially the morale and meaning of your story in your audience's mind.

The Imperial Stormtrooper commandment

This is a biggie. Remember all those guys in white stormtrooper uniforms in *Star Wars*? And remember what you felt when Luke or Han Solo shot them and they died?

Nothing! You felt nothing, because you didn't know them. Beyond them even being bad guys, they are faceless, nameless creatures. As a result, you have no connection to them and no strong emotional response to their deaths.

So, then, how does this apply to your storytelling?

Well, if something bad happens to your nameless antagonist, don't worry about it. But if you want us to feel for the protagonist in your story when something bad happens to them, we need to meet them, know them, and emotionally connect to them before they face adversity. In other words, if you want us to really care about a person, let us meet them first, before you have events transpire that affect them.

The Passover principle

In the traditional Jewish holiday of Passover, one is asked to think about the story of Moses and the Israelites' exodus from Egypt. This story is read every year and questions are asked to help those at the table relate to this story and how it applies to their lives today.

My favorite line in the whole Passover service asks, "How is this night different from all other nights?"

In fact, I like this line so much that I have rephrased it and have used it with all of my students. If you work with me in class, your story must pass the Passover principle and you must be able to answer the question "How is your story different from all other stories?"

Of course, all stories will inevitably share some structural similarities, but it is imperative that you, as a writer, think about making your story different.

What specific elements can you employ and must you utilize to differentiate your story from every other story ever written? Sure, it's a bit overwhelming, but it's your job!

The been there, done that directive

A corollary to the Passover principle is this one. When you look at your story, are there any scenes, events, or lines of dialogue that feel false or overly familiar or just plain predictable? Have we already "been there and done that"?

If so, they must be trashed and new, more original language should be inserted.

The baby on a high window sill injunction

When you have a tense moment, such as a baby crawling along a window sill 12 stories up, you want to always think about extending the scene instead of curtailing it.

Your goal when you have a good moment of suspense is to stretch it out. Audiences love these kinds of moments and most writers tend to end them a bit too quickly. Always consider how you can have the baby slip a little, and then a little bit more, and extend the moment to last as long as dramatically possible.

The old Mr. Withers/Scooby Doo directive

Endings are always tricky. There is a tendency for endings to be too simplistic and for far too much explaining to occur. Endings are also hugely important. If you screw up the ending of your story, no matter how good the rest of your story is, you will have failed and the audience will be let down. So, when considering your ending, think about the Old Mr. Withers/Scooby Doo directive. Let me explain:

In most every episode of the old cartoon TV series *Scooby Doo*, the ghost/monster/ demon/beast is unmasked and revealed to just be old Mr. Withers who wanted to scare everybody away so he could have all the land cheap and sell it for a huge profit. Upon revealing that the ghost/monster/demon/beast is not real and just old Mr. Withers, usually it is Velma, the smart, more "nerdy-looking" one of the gang who explains to all exactly how old Mr. Withers pulled it all off.

So, what can we learn from this? Well, first be careful of an overly simplistic ending in which everything is revealed too easily. Once you do have a reveal at the end, be careful of having everybody in your story standing around and listening as you or your Velma tries to explain it all to them.

Audiences have become very sophisticated, and these days they will quickly see what is really happening. Let them write the ending in their head, and make sure that ending is satisfying to them and need not be explained. They will get the moral of your story if your story is told well!

The shark in your tank decree

This is one of my favorites. It is derived from a story I heard about the fish stick industry. I am not sure if it is true or apocryphal, but in the end, it's a great story, so I don't really care. So here goes.

The head of a fish stick company was in trouble. Consumers were complaining that his fish sticks did not taste as fresh as they should. Sales were down and he didn't know what to do. Concerned, he brought live fish into the factory so that they would be happily swimming around in a tank until the very last moment when they would be processed into fish sticks.

Still, the fish sticks tasted, well, not so fresh. At wit's end, the owner was ready to throw in the towel when the janitor of the factory walked up to him and said that he was an avid fisherman and he had an idea. The owner was desperate, so he readily agreed to listen. The janitor suggested that they drop a few little sand sharks into the tank. This caused all the fish in the tank to swim around like crazy as they were constantly being pursued by the sharks.

And just in the moment after the fish escaped the sharks, they were captured and processed into fish sticks. The taste difference was huge. Finally, the fish sticks tasted incredibly fresh, and the meat was tender and firm, and sales soared.

So, what's the meaning of this tale? In my mind, it's a great parable about how in most of our stories, we are happy to have our characters swimming around lazily. What we need to do every time we write, is to think of how we can drop more sharks into our story. This way we crank up the stakes so that our characters are desperately swimming through life and the story feels as if it's filled with great tension, complicated action, and life!

The catalyst canon

In general, most stories start with a situation that is dysfunctional and out of balance. You were in trouble, or your business was hurting and you needed to make changes or else. Then, suddenly, a catalyst—a new product, a new system, something different—is introduced and the story really *takes off!*

This is the "catalyst canon." The beginning of the story is essentially the old status quo, and then it is problematic. The story then kicks into high gear as the catalyst is introduced. And then, when all the conflict has been resolved, the story reaches a satisfying denouement and a new status quo has been reached. Amen!

The glazed donut truth

The last but not least rule/tool that I want to mention is a simple one. Before I share my work, I always ask myself: Are there any moments in this story when the audience's eyes will glaze over like a hot donut?

You must be brutal with your own work. If something in your story is not necessary, get rid of it. And no matter how good your beginning is, if the middle or end moves slowly, you are in trouble. Be judicious with what you include in your story.

A final checklist

Lastly, you might want to check this one out and see if your story does the following. Note, however, it must do *all* the following for your audience, not just for you:

1. Does it entertain?
2. Does it inform or teach?
3. Does it engage or connect?
4. Does it tap into emotions?
5. Does it feel genuine?
6. Does it employ specifics?
7. Does it use as many senses as possible?
8. Can it be shorter, tighter, better?

Part 3: Narrative Typologies

CHAPTER 11

Origin/Background Stories

||||||||||||||||||||||||||||||||||||||||||||||||||||||||||||||||||||||||||||||||||||||||||||||||||||||||||||||||||||||||||||||||||||||||||||||||||||||||||||||||||||||||

The most important things to remember about
back story are that (a) everyone has a history
and (b) most of it isn't very interesting.
—Stephen King, *On Writing: A Memoir of the Craft*

On a core level, stories work because they are non-hierarchical. In other words, they provide an inoffensive way to push forward your agenda. I see many types of business narratives being used on a daily basis. The following types of stories are the most prevalent. Can you think of examples that fit each of these?

Note that I usually urge my clients to really polish one good personal signature story that they can use in a multitude of situations. This is your go-to story, the one that embodies one or more of the following typologies.

This is probably something deeply personal; it is your story, an authentic piece of your life, told to illustrate who you are and your connection to your company or brand. The personal experience you relate in this story both defines you and connects you to your brand or company. It can be told by a CEO, executive, manager, employee, staff member, or consumer. And your signature story can be any or even all of the following:

Origin Story: This story relates the beginnings of your company to the world. In doing so, it allows the consumer to better understand who you are and your core values in an inoffensive way.

Mission/Purpose/Values Story: The content of this narrative may contain just about any story, but its theme and meaning are designed specifically to transfer core values and/or a mission/purpose that the brand or company want to embody.

Knowledge/Information Story: This story allows the wisdom and collective knowledge of the company culture to be stored and transferred to new people who are joining the company and will be essential to its success.

Brand/Product Vision Myth: This is a biggie. It is an inspiring story that tends to ignite passion and helps the company progress through the difficulty of any transition. In relating a vision for the future, this narrative provides an emotional blueprint for people in the company and for clients and customers who purchase from the company as they deal with change.

In this chapter, I will focus exclusively on the origin story and then, in the following chapters, we will look at other types of stories, when to use them, and so on.

Origin stories

Who are you as a company and why are you here? Your origin story does more than just tell about where you came from; it also informs where you are going and communicates who you are along the way.

Take the company United Services Automobile Association (USAA). If you go to their Website, they urge you to become part of the USAA family and they claim they will be there for you during every stage of your life. They offer to help you with insurance, banking, investments, and retirement. They tell you that it's free to join and if you are unsure, you can rest assured based upon their origin story:

"Our story is built on the values you live by. USAA began in 1922, when twenty-five Army officers agreed to insure each other's vehicles when no one else would. Today we follow the same military values our founders prized: service, loyalty, honesty and integrity."

It is a simple story that stresses their humble beginnings and their values. To be honest, I wish they said more about their beginnings and established who they are a bit more, but it's a good start.

Next, I'd like to explore a company that has effectively discovered their Brand DNA and, as result, they've created a series of brand narratives that has led to great success. It's an organization that is well-aligned and it's a place where everyone knows, feels, lives, and breathes their Brand DNA.

The company I'd like to look at is Uno Alla Volta, which means "one at a time." Their tagline is "from the hearts and hands of artisans." Their CEO is Terri Alpert, and I should reveal here that I went to high school with Terri and am hugely proud of how successful she has become. I just think it's incredible that she has created a socially conscious, multi-million-dollar business from her home in a few decades with just a small initial investment. Uno Alla Volta is famous for its gorgeous catalogs, even in this age of the Internet. Terri told me that 50 percent of her transactions do come in online, but her beautiful catalogs drive 10 times more business to her Website than social media does.

Terri says that "These days, almost everyone needs at least two of the three channels: bricks and mortar, Web, print." With Uno Alla Volta, she has focused on Web and print. In essence, Uno Alla Volta is a direct marketer that specializes in selling handmade jewelry and crafts.

On their Website, they describe themselves this way:

Talk to our artisans, and you will hear in their voices the happiness that creation can bring. They will speak of the joy of spreading "particles" of their human spirit throughout the world, much as a dandelion spreads its seeds. You will hear of their wish to create something truly lasting—something which will be cherished, appreciated, and shared.

Talk to our customers and they will share with you an appreciation of what it means to be a caretaker of work fashioned by a fellow human being. You will hear that when they come to Uno Alla Volta, they are welcomed into our *una grande famiglia*, our one great big family.

Talk to those who have received gifts carefully chosen for them and you will hear how wonderful it is to receive creations from the hearts and hands of artisans. They will tell you how special it is to know a bit about the life of the artisan and how the personalized certificates of authenticity forever serve as a reminder of the human connection—the dear friend or family member who gave them the gift, the artisan who crafted it and the great many people here who made it all happen.

This is good writing and good storytelling. Terri ends this mission statement with this quote: "Talk to me and you will hear how I have found my true calling in this life. You will hear of my never-ending gratitude for the gift of being able to facilitate the creativity and growth of so many. And, to whom do I owe that gratitude? I owe it to all of you—*la mia famiglia*—my family—*mia una grande famiglia!*"

I love their catalogs and am convinced that to sell their handicrafts, they are really selling stories. Take these scissors, for example:

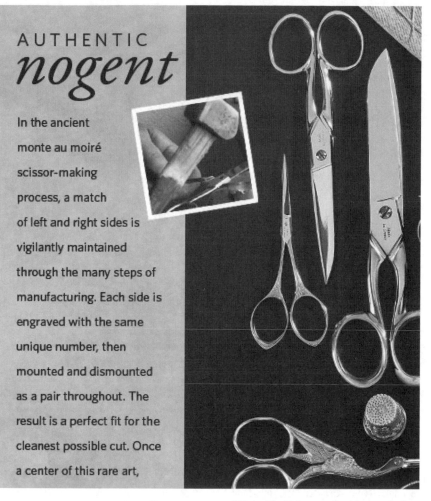

AUTHENTIC
nogent

In the ancient monte au moiré scissor-making process, a match of left and right sides is vigilantly maintained through the many steps of manufacturing. Each side is engraved with the same unique number, then mounted and dismounted as a pair throughout. The result is a perfect fit for the cleanest possible cut. Once a center of this rare art,

Image courtesy of Uno Alla Volta, used with permission.

The story makes you salivate over a pair of scissors. I never wanted one before, but now—I can't help it—I am dying for a pair. Or take this jewelry:

MEET OUR DESIGNER
Yvonne

Yvonne's career as a flight attendant frequently brought her to Asia. Over two decades ago, she became so enthralled with the life stories of Tibetan refugees and with their magnificent beadwork that she gave up her career in the sky to create a fair trade business.

Discover Now ▶

Image courtesy of Uno Alla Volta, used with permission.

I am hooked. I want that jewelry because of the story behind the jewelry.

The stories being told are so interesting that they make you want to buy the product. And it's easy to forget, but images, such as photos, tell stories too! Terri even told me, "My photographers know that they are storytellers. They ask the merchants what kind of emotion we are going for and then they have to nail it...while still showing all the physical attributes accurately."

Beyond the stories told in the catalog, the origin story of how Uno Alla Volta came into being is a good one. So now, I will get to the interview and let Terri tell it to you and I hope you will soon see how it's a key element to their brand as a whole:

RK: Can you give us your origin story?

TA: Okay, you asked for it so here it is:

In 1993, I was a Wall Street tech maven with a degree in physics, who was on my maternity leave after having just given birth to my daughter Sarah. Now remember: This was an era when entrepreneurship was decidedly not cool, and risk-taking was considered crazy. So, in a way, starting a family actually gave me a "leg up" over many male would-be entrepreneurs, as "maternity leave" created a level of safety for me, or so I felt. In other words, it actually reduced (even if only in my mind) the risk of failure by reducing the stigma of failure. You see, after all, even if my new business project was a flop, I could always justify it as something I tried for fun during my time away from Wall Street.

The truth is that for all my skills, financial knowledge, technical know-how, and project management expertise, I knew I didn't know "squat" about running a business, let alone creating one from scratch. So I framed my first venture as a "science experiment," a learning exercise. To both minimize my family's financial risk, and to maximize my learning, I allocated myself only $10,000 in startup capital. I vowed that whatever I learned, it would be by trial and error on the cheap. And because I was a scientist, I wanted to develop a business in which results were measurable and repeatable.

I sensed that some type of "mail order" business, as direct marketing was called back in the day, might just be the right business model. It would provide a national audience from day one. The 800 number could even ring in my home without anyone ever knowing that this was a home business.

By selling to consumers, there would be no accounts receivables. If I could find a way to turn my inventory faster than I had to pay for it, perhaps I could use normal trade terms of net 30 to help finance my marketing efforts. This would work if I had to find a product line in which I could offer the world's best selection, along with the world's most knowledgeable service. But what?

Terri's first light-bulb moment

I was home with my six-month-old colicky daughter who had only two modes: nursing and screaming. I was dealing with my own post-partum depression, and the loss of professional identity, and so, frankly, one day I just lost my shit!

My husband could tell something was wrong and so he came home early to give me a much-needed break. He then suggested, "Hey, let's all go for a ride."

I grabbed the baby and we drove around. We had no place special in mind and so when we saw a restaurant supply shop that had a sign on the front that said, "Public Welcome," we decided to give it a try. Ten minutes later, after browsing through the store, both my husband and I looked at each other and said, "Found it!"

High-end kitchen knives. Yep, high-end kitchen knives!

At this time, really good knives were not easy to find, so I had found my niche. A few months later, Professional Cutlery Direct was born. I took out my first advertisement in *Food and Wine Magazine*. A full week before I thought the magazine would even be seen, the 800 number rang, and I sold my first knife. I picked up now 10-month-old baby Sarah and clutched her to my chest and jumped up and down with delight, exclaiming, "We're in BID-ness, Sarah Bear. We're in BID-ness!"

I was fully aware that the value of my business at any time was a simple function of the quality of each customer's most recent experience. So I put a lot of thought into how I would shape each experience. For example, I insisted there be a handwritten note on every packing slip forever, a practice we continue to this day.

I hired and trained customer service associates who could provide an incredibly high level of dedicated, knowledgeable service. I brought the owners of the factories that made many of America and Europe's finest culinary tools to Connecticut to do show-and-tell sessions with my employees, educating them on the tools, their construction, their use, and the origin stories of their own companies.

I encouraged my service associates to leverage the human connection when talking with customers. If a customer was asking a question about a Wusthof knife, the associate might say, "Well that's a really good question. In fact, I asked a very similar question myself to Wolfgang Wusthof, when he was here last August." Now at that point, the customer realizes they are talking to someone who has personally spoken with the owner of the most prestigious knife company in the world. There's credibility.

Yet it has to be done with the right touch. There can't be hubris, just a reminder that every one of us puts our pants on one leg at a time. Again and again, I reminded my team, "Remember: People don't buy from companies, they buy from people!"

Over the next several years, Professional Cutlery Direct grew rapidly, always profitably, and it was financed entirely from internally generated cash flow. There was a slight slowdown in growth in 1996, the year I gave birth to my second daughter, Rachel. Nonetheless, the company achieved $1,000,000 in sales that year and within another three years it was selling $10,000,000 in knives, cookware, and other core hand tools to serious hobby cooks around the country. All along the way, I kept thinking, "This is much too easy."

And, I have "absolutely nothing protectable."

Remember: This was to be just a science experiment. I didn't expect it to work. Yet it was working and in order to continue, the company was going to need a building and need a management team. So, at long last, I took the plunge, making major investments that required serious debt.

Winning awards for growth (three-time winner of the Inc. 500 for being among the fastest-growing private companies in the nation, the Cisco Growing Technology Award, the Award of Excellence from the International Association of Culinary Professionals, and even being named Entrepreneur of the Year by Business New Haven), anyone on the outside would say, "Hey, that company is healthy and going places." In fact, anyone who looked at the financial statements would also see a very rosy picture. But I wasn't looking at the financial statements. Those, I knew, were nothing more than a rear-view mirror. My eyes were fixed squarely on the road ahead and I didn't like what I was seeing.

My current profits were due to my building of the customer base over many, many years, and it was costing me more and more to acquire new customers who seemed to be worth less and less.

Why? The world was changing rapidly, and now every big box store and every new dotcom was offering the products, which were previously very hard to find. Customers and competitors were looking to Professional Cutlery Direct (PCD) to know what the top products were, to understand how to use them, but then many of them were buying them elsewhere.

In fact, one customer told my customer associates that she used to work in a Williams-Sonoma store and when she was trained there, she was told that when a customer there had a question she couldn't answer, she should call PCD for the answer. Yikes!

PCD was building demand for these great products but in doing so, it was building the business for its suppliers and its competitors. And, now PCD had a management team, we had a 30,000-square-foot facility, we had technology infrastructure, and we had *debt!* Our ship was heading right toward an iceberg.

So now what? I knew it was time for a change, but what would be my next step?

As I kept thinking about all the things right with the PCD business model and all the things wrong with it, I decided to do what I always do in times of crisis: make some lists. My lists led to the development of criteria— criteria that would comprise the ideal attributes for a new catalog company that would leverage the existing infrastructure I already had.

My big criteria:

- A meaningful brand. Check. Professional Cutlery Direct was so meaningful that when I asked customers how they had heard about us, most said that they had been buying from us for years.
- Category flexibility. But PCD was a confining brand. We were such an authority on cutlery that we didn't even have the same credibility for cookware. The meaning was much too functional, much too narrow. I needed a brand that would allow the business to adapt to the types of products our customers would want to buy. Therefore, a meaningful brand needed to be emotionally meaningful not functionally meaningful.
- Proprietary product. PCD was selling items that were available elsewhere. A new brand would have to have proprietary product so that as it developed customer loyalty, the customers would be loyal to my company and not my supplier's.
- Barriers to entry. Whatever the next brand was, it couldn't be easy to replicate. I had to create something protectable for it to have any lasting value.

With these criteria/attributes in hand, I took a fresh look inward and asked myself: What brings me joy? What truly nourishes my soul?

I also took a fresh look at my merchandising data. What were all those petri dishes containing my science experiments telling me? Hmm...

The answer was clear. The best-performing products that PCD had were ones that were handcrafted, and for which I was telling their story: French pocket knives and beautifully painted Polish pottery.

My second light-bulb moment

A-ha! That's it. Handcrafted products. Not products, really. Treasures. Treasures made by artisans. Treasures made one at a time. Treasures touched by the human spirit with great stories to tell. Such a brand would meet all of the criteria! And with the French pocket knives and the Polish Pottery, there was a place to start. Now what could possibly connect these two? Hmm...ah! Venetian glass.

And so, in 2002, I launched a test catalog built around this core. In the very first catalog, I told my customers that each treasure would be accompanied by its story. I aimed to create stories that you would remember after reading the catalog. And if you were giving the product as a gift, would the gift recipient know it is as special as you do? So, I created little cards with stories that would go with each product. Yes, each product line was its own little science experiment.

And thank goodness I didn't wait a moment longer because, at that moment, I was coming face to face with that big iceberg. All my fears about selling branded products in the age of the Internet and box stores were coming true, yet even faster than I ever expected. Running both companies from the one infrastructure created more than a little chaos. But I needed PCD to bring in the dollars to cover the cost of my infrastructure and I needed to keep the infrastructure in order to be able to grow Uno Alla Volta (UAV). This was how I steered my ship and avoided that big iceberg.

Fast-forward to 2006, and UAV is on fire; PCD is much smaller, is now called *Cooking Enthusiast*, and is still ticking. Almost too good to be true. Once again, it is time to make significant investments in infrastructure to support the next level of growth. It is time to take this two-brand enterprise from $20,000,000 in revenues to something many times larger. To accomplish this goal, I would need a serious management team. Costly for a few years, but necessary; and it will be well worth it in the end, or so I told myself. It didn't turn out that way, of course. Instead, I found myself facing another iceberg. I'll skip a few chapters, but let's just say that I am truly grateful that we survived to write new chapters of our story, and that our best chapters are still yet to come.

RK: Beyond your origin story, please tell me all about the other kinds of stories you use and why you use them?

TA: Well, let's see. There are many stories baked into my leadership style. I run a lot of "town meetings," which we call "State of the UNO." I use these to help create the ongoing narrative, which binds my team together, to psyche them up, and to understand both our common vision and the inner workings of our economic engine, so that they can each use their own native genius to advance our common goals.

I find stories to be layers. They interconnect, intertwine. There are stories about stories and there are stories that give context to stories. For me, the act of writing is such a one-dimensional, linear, sequential task. And the stories? That, I see in my mind, are two-dimensional or even three-dimensional. So when I first put pen to paper, I tend to overdo it and weave in and out. But I need to write that way to let all the words out. Then, I step back and revise all that content in order to make a compelling *polished* story.

By the way, in addition to "stories," my communication style is always metaphorical. I might refer to "starter yeast" if I know someone has culinary background or use "field" analogies with an athlete, etc. It really sucks, though, that I couldn't play a sport or a musical instrument if my life depended on it. So I never know if I'm messing up my metaphors. I certainly mix them all the time. One paragraph could have cooking, music, film editing, and football in it.

Overall, I think there are many kinds of stories that I use:

1. Stories about our artisans for our customers.
2. Stories about me for our customers.
3. Stories about our customers for each other; stories about our customers for our artisans. (It all links together.)
4. Stories about Uno Alla Volta evolving from Professional Cutlery Direct.

RK: Give me an example of a specific story or stories that you are most proud of?

TA: Well, let me start with a cool biz factoid: Our results improved measurably when I started sharing aspects of my life and philosophy of living with our customers. It brings the authenticity to the brand. So we decided to try something new in 2014. Instead of some form of site-wide discount or some pushing of excess inventory, we built our Cyber Monday special around "A few of my favorite things" and it was a huge hit. The sales happened not because of price, but only because of the *human connection* our customers made with me and my life/philosophy, etc. Again, proof that storytelling works! We did so much better with this as our Cyber Monday special than we would have by just giving away margin on current product or trying to put another spin on 50 percent off of "leftovers."

Every issue of our catalog, 15 a year, now begins with a unique letter from me, connecting our brand philosophy with the season or with a particular product line. They get really personal. Boy, when I first started sharing personal stuff with our readers/consumers, was I nervous! I just felt so vulnerable and so uncomfortable being this vulnerable with half a million strangers! Here is the specific text to give you a feel for it:

Why blue?

From the earliest moments of childhood, blue has been my favorite color. Today, at nearly 52 years of age, I have figured out why. I am a very high energy person, moving, thinking, planning, and creating almost all the time. Those who know and love me adore my passion, but abhor the tension that comes from my more frenetic behaviors.

Cobalt and ocean blues remind me of family summer vacations in the Outer Banks. They take me back to the beach, sitting by the ocean, and watching the waves lap up onto the sand as the sun sets and hints of sapphire and dusk dance across the darkening sky. Surrounding myself with these hues is calming. They remind me to slow down, to breathe slowly. To stop creating. To stop doing. To stop talking. To simply be.

Why spirals?

I love the grace of a meandering line, the cyclical nature of a circle broken out of infinite repetition and into the forward direction. For me, the spiral is a metaphor for life. Each year, as the seasons pass, and as the birthdays come around, I want to make sure that I have grown and become a better me.

Why interconnecting circles?

The circle for me is a symbol of friends and family. How often do we each speak about those in our inner circle? We all have our circles of influence which expand ever outwards beginning with our own souls, then our immediate family, then our extended family and dear friends, followed by our neighborhoods, our churches, our synagogues, and, ultimately, all of those with whom we share this beautiful planet.

When these human connections begin to overlap, those are, for me, those linked circles. So if you come to Uno Alla Volta seeking the perfect gift for someone dear in your life, in your inner circle, you are then linking with the inner circle of the artisan who crafted the treasure, and the inner circle of every member of our una grande famiglia—Uno Alla Volta's one big family. All our lives are now inextricably linked to one another even if only in the smallest of ways.

Why labradorite?

It is a soft spoken neutral with fire within! Its iridescence is magical. It changes with each glance, yet in an oh-so-subtle way. If opal and dichroic glass shout "Look at me sparkle! Let me light up the room!" then labradorite whispers "I am to be appreciated by those who care to pay attention. I know who I am. I like who I am. And you will find me here long after the show is over and the lights have dimmed."

Why lapis and sapphire?

It is those deep blue hues again, beckoning me, pulling me into the water, and offering me their oasis of calm.

And garnet?

To celebrate my birth (January) and, thus, my life. It is a deep, calm, noble red, not at all showy like the bright, bold ruby.

RK: Why have you chosen to embrace both stories about your artisans and products, but also bigger UAV brand stories?

TA: Stories, in all their forms—words and pictures, textures, memories, and emotions—are a vehicle for conveying our humanity and for making the essential connections with one another that define our lives. Stories are one of the primary ways we have of striving to achieve the Uno Alla Volta vision, which is "To bring the human connection into every interaction with every customer, artisan, coworker, and supplier—thereby enriching their lives. By so doing, we enrich each of our own lives as well."

Now then, you may ask, "Why are stories at the heart of Uno Alla Volta?" Because, quite simply, we don't sell "stuff." We sell treasures crafted by the hands and shaped by the hearts of artisans. I ask you, Rich: How can one have a proper appreciation of what is in your hand, if you don't have a sense of where it comes from and why and how it came into being?

Whether they are silversmiths in California, glass blowers in Venice, ceramicists in Poland, our artisans speak of the profound joy that comes from knowing that they are creating an object that will bring joy to someone halfway across the world, someone they will never meet. And, they speak of the hope that long after they themselves are no longer on this earth, items created from their imagination, crafted by their hands, and touched by their spirit will continue to put smiles on the faces of others.

So Rich, let's say you see a beautiful necklace in our catalog that you know your mother will love. In that moment, you've made a connection. Our artisan's design pulled at you and touched you. When you present your mom with her gift, sure she may "ooh" and "aah" at how pretty it is, but if that's all that happens, then this necklace is just another thing. But say, instead, she understands just a small bit about the person who created the necklace, and all those who facilitated this moment. Well then, her appreciation for the work in her hands is all the greater. Perhaps even she may view herself less as its owner than its caretaker. In her hands is the creative work of a fellow traveler in life's journey.

At Uno Alla Volta, we have an obligation to tell these stories.

CHAPTER 12

Mission/Purpose/ Values Stories

||||||||||||||||||||||||||||||||||||||||||||||||||||||||||||||||||||||||||||||||||||||||||||||||||||||||||||||||||||||||||||||||||||||||||||

*It's not hard to make decisions when you
know what your values are.*

—Roy Disney

Stories can work to convey the values that you want your company to possess and the mission that you want your company to pursue. Hence, your story might also be working as a sort of living embodiment of your mission statement. But be careful: As I've discussed over and over again in the previous pages, the story must correspond to the core Brand DNA and must convey the proper messaging along the right brand lines.

Let's take an interesting example. *My Dad's Story—Dream for My Child* is a very moving short film made for MetLife Hong Kong. It tells the story of a man who loves his daughter so much that he does everything in his power to give her a good life. But he lies to her about having a steady job and having money. In the end, the daughter's voiceover essentially reveals that the she knows that her daddy loves her so much that he has fabricated lies in order to try to keep her happy and blissfully unaware.

The quality of the storytelling and the emotional power of the story are both unquestionable. Yet, I still wonder about this kind of brand storytelling. Does it fit with the brand? Does it sell more life insurance? Does it help connect you to MetLife? Go to YouTube and watch it, and see what you think.

Let me give you another example. This one is about using a story in a business meeting to help solidify things with a client. The story goes like this. My brother is an executive creative director with a big advertising agency. He has worked for many big agencies and many famous brands. In every meeting with a new brand, it's his job to show the clients that he "gets their brand."

One day, he was in a business meeting with his new Gillette clients and they were trying to define their brand. They asked him who he thought best personifies their brand. Was it a movie star like George Clooney? Sean Connery? Brad Pitt?

He suggested maybe a story would be a better way to define Gillette as more of a confident, yet humble, cool-under-pressure kind of brand. The story he told was about one of his heroes, a man who represented the ultimate Joe Cool: Joe Montana.

It was Super Bowl XXIII. The seconds were ticking down. Cincinnati was winning, but the San Francisco 49ers, led by quarterback Joe Montana, were moving down the field. The players' hearts were pounding, the fans were holding onto their seats. One of Montana's teammates said he came back into the huddle and looked at the team's leader, Montana, waiting to see how he was dealing with the pressure. They knew they would live or die by their quarterback.

Would he be sweating? Would he be freaking out? Would he be throwing up (like a certain quarterback from Philadelphia was reputed to have done)?

Just then, Montana looked up at his teammates, gestured over to the sidelines, pointed into the crowd, and said, "Hey, is that comedian John Candy up there in the stands? Wow! That's awesome."

Montana seemed almost blissfully unaware of the fact that hundreds of millions of people were watching this, the biggest football game of the year, and there were only a few seconds left and if they failed, they would lose.

Montana cared about none of that. He was being himself and being cool. One of his favorite movie stars was watching him right now and he got a kick out of that. He wasn't stressed. He wasn't worried. He knew that he could do what needed to be done to win the game and he wanted to enjoy the moment.

It was then that the rest of the team stopped being worried. It was then that they knew they would win.

And they did.

This story helped the client gain a deeper understanding of their brand, as well as give them a deeper sense of trust in my brother as the creative director who would bring their brand to life on television in their next advertising campaign.

And he did.

‖‖‖‖‖‖‖‖‖‖‖‖‖‖‖‖‖‖‖‖‖‖‖

Next up, I was able to speak with Michael Simon, chief marketing Officer of Bai Brands, who is a master of delivering fresh brand narratives and has done creative and fantastic work with brands such as Pepperidge Farm, Campbell's Soup, Godiva Chocolates, and Panera Bread. Michael is an incredibly busy guy, but he was gracious enough to spend a few minutes listening to my questions and then offering these answers relating to how mission/purpose/value stories can help a brand or company.

RK: What role do you see storytelling playing in branding and marketing today?

MS: A marketer aspires to drive a deep and emotional connection with his or her customer. I describe it as moving the customer from preference to love. Storytelling is a device that enables deeper and more memorable engagement often built on a shared sense of values. To break through in today's cluttered world of 24/7 messaging, a brand must be able to differentiate itself and allow people to understand what it truly stands for. Storytelling is a very effective means to engage, educate, and build affinity with your customers.

RK: How do you create, cultivate, and sustain lifelong relationships with customers via digital narratives across all forms of media?

MS: I think it starts with a foundational understanding of what needs a consumer is trying to satisfy with your product or service; in the words of Harvard Business School professor Clay Christensen, knowing the job the customer is hiring you to complete.

But I think it goes even deeper. While people seek products and services to satisfy a functional need, it often ladders up to something more emotional and human. Southwest Airlines was more than simply a low-cost airline. It was providing the 85 percent of the U.S. population who couldn't afford airline travel when Southwest was founded, the freedom to fly, which enabled greater connection in those people's lives.

The world of marketing has evolved from informing and selling consumers about the benefits of your product or service to connecting and conversing with the customer. A great brand always sees themselves through the lens of their customer. You must understand how a brand can offer value to their lives. Without that understanding, your communication becomes just another forgettable amalgamation of words in the sea of messages consumers are bombarded with each and every day. While fundamental, that depth of knowledge represents just the beginning.

In a world where every brand is vying for love and attention, the articulation of a brand's values and soul are equally important. Creating a narrative that delivers meaningful content wrapped in the DNA of your brand becomes paramount to building relationships. This narrative is not limited to one channel. It must be fully integrated across all consumer touch points. It must be consistent and come from a singular voice and point of view. We live in an omni-channel world with people utilizing multiple devices throughout the day to obtain information and enable connection.

Being clear on your brand narrative and the role of each channel in telling your story is critical. In addition, listening to your customer becomes as important as informing them. When you have a message that resonates with the consumer and you share and express that message in a relevant and compelling way, you are well on your way to cultivating and sustaining lifelong relationships with your customers, evolving those interactions with them from transactional to transformational.

RK: It is said that it is not just about storytelling anymore, but about timeless, ever-evolving brand narratives that you must create and control. Do you agree and, if so, can you comment?

MS: I don't think it was ever just about storytelling. Storytelling was simply a device to deliver the message. What you stand for as a brand (your brand essence or brand narrative) is the foundation that drives everything. The key to establishing deep, sustaining relationships with your customers is to connect with them around a set of shared values, not just a story.

However, a story with no substance will soon be forgotten the moment it is completed. The Bible is a series of stories that speak to a set of core values and a philosophy on life. These tenets or principles are continually reinforced across thousands of years. People remember the stories, but are connected to the ideals.

RK: Marketing used to be about creating a myth and selling it; now it is about finding a truth and sharing it. We are moving from storytelling to brand narratives. So what exactly are brand narratives?

MS: To me, a brand narrative is the essence and soul of a brand. It's why the brand exists. A good exercise is to ask: What would the world lose if your brand did not exist?

The answer to that question is an effective way to truly understand if your brand stands for anything. If the world would lose nothing, the brand never stood for anything in the first place. In Simon Sinek's great book *Start With Why*, he examines companies who are built on a core purpose, their "why," versus those companies that tell you "what" they do. "Why"-based companies have been shown, across a number of longitudinal studies, to generate greater performance, more engaged employees, and more loyal customers.

When you can connect with someone through the heart rather than just the head, you create a relationship, not a transaction. I firmly believe people want to be inspired. They seek ways to enrich their lives. In a world where myth has become the emperor with no clothes, authenticity is what reigns supreme. Authenticity is built on honesty, transparency, and soul—all critical ingredients of a brand narrative.

RK: What kinds of stories do you use and why? Any and all specific examples that you can share will be much appreciated.

MS: I think of a good story having—as described by Jim Signorelli in his book *StoryBranding*—a character (or characters) dealing with obstacles to achieve certain goals. The extent to which stories help us connect with our own truths is a function of how well we can identify with the values, beliefs, and feelings experienced by its character.

In the consumer world, the main character is the consumer who represents the protagonist. They are faced with obstacles that prevent them from satisfying either a functional or emotional need. The brand, through both its functional capabilities and its fundamental beliefs, enables the customer-protagonist to overcome these barriers and achieve its goals.

The brand is trying to build, not force, a relationship with the customer. A story is an effective way for a brand to connect with its customers around a set of shared values and ideals, the critical step in forging a relationship built on a strong emotional bond.

In my own experience, I think of my time at Pepperidge Farm, Inc., and the Goldfish story represents to me a great example of the power of applying story as a means of articulating core purpose. Goldfish is a brand built on optimism. Optimism is defined as having a positive outlook on life. An optimistic person does not fall victim to life's unexpected obstructions, but rather uses their creativity to overcome those obstacles.

There are a host of academic studies that show that people who possess a more positive outlook on life live happier, healthier, and more enriching lives. Academic studies also show that one is not born with an optimistic attitude toward life. It can be nurtured and learned. The articulation of this philosophy of optimism for children was told through the context of entertainment. The story of "Finn and Friends," two Goldfish crackers that came to life, showcased a cast of compelling animated characters who engaged in a variety of fun adventures always believing that they could overcome any obstacles they faced.

For all the moms out there, we developed a brand narrative called "Fishful Thinking." This program offered information and exercises for Mom to share with her children to help teach them to develop and reinforce a mindful optimism—that there was no challenge that couldn't be successfully confronted. These life lessons were the key to enabling their children's short-term and long-term happiness—moms' #1 aspiration for their kids as revealed through a Gallup survey we conducted. Every channel, from traditional to digital to earned media to owned media, was used to engage our target with this brand narrative.

RK: How do you use stories to emotionally differentiate any brand from all of the others in the same category and how has storytelling moved toward brand narratives told by many creators and constantly revised by consumers in different forms of digital communication and social media?

MS: The key to creating emotional differentiation relative to competition is to uncover the purpose of the brand that speaks to its core essence. It must be authentic to the brand and not feel derivative of anyone else.

In her terrific book, *Different*, Young Me Moon of the Harvard Business School describes that great brands of the future must answer these four questions:

"What do we promise that nobody else in our industry can promise?"

"What do we deliver that nobody else can deliver?"

"What do we believe that only we believe?"

"In a world of abundance, what do we offer that is scarce?"

To truly build emotional differentiation, you must find a core truth endemic to your brand ("What do you offer that is scarce?") that also strikes true to your core audience. The story becomes the means to convey your brand narrative and foster both awareness and understanding.

It begins by sharing it with like-minded individuals. However, if your brand narrative speaks to a real human truth, it eventually becomes no longer your truth, but is shared with a community of those who espouse similar beliefs and values. This is where digital and social media play an important role. They become the interface that facilitates conversation and content around these shared ideals throughout your community. Your relationship with your customer evolves from "you to them" to "you and them" or "us."

RK: Do you have a specific process in which you craft brand narratives that you would be willing to share with readers?

MS: I've employed a process that starts with identifying what I call the Energy Driving Idea (EDI) of a brand. The EDI is the essential strategic idea that defines the soul of the brand and drives the brand's communication. It is action-oriented and purposeful. The EDI grounds and inspires what we say and helps guide how we further articulate this idea and drive communication strategy and architecture. The EDI is defined as the intersection of the barrier and the brand essence:

The Barrier → EDI ← The Brand Essence
There is a simple process to arrive at the EDI.
Step 1: Situational analysis.
Step 2: Reducing it down to the behavioral challenge.
Step 3: Understanding the behavioral target.
Step 4: Barrier analysis to understand what obstacles inhibit the desired behavior.
Step 5: Business brief (develop communication strategy that articulates the over-arching business issue and goals that brand narrative will address, providing deep insights into target motivators and touch points within competitive and marketplace context).
Step 6: The energy driving idea (a singular idea that is the strategic springboard for a creative idea and contextual framework that will release and direct the energy in a brand).

Once you identify the EDI, the agency or creative team must then frame the story in a compelling and memorable way to share the brand's ethos with the world. The story must connect the main characters (the brand and the target).

In the short term ("the dating phase"), the brand will help satisfy the needs of the target by enabling the customer, through its functional attributes and their benefits, to achieve its goals. Long term, the story must spark a flame that connects the brand and the consumer around a core set of shared values and beliefs. The story itself dramatizes the obstacles that the consumer must confront and how the brand helps the target face and ultimately overcome these hurdles leading to the establishment of a deep relationship between target and brand. The extent to which any of these obstacles must be overcome sets up the plot.

CHAPTER 13

Knowledge/Information Based Stories

‖‖

No thief, however skillful, can rob one of knowledge, and that
is why knowledge is the best and safest treasure to acquire.
— L. Frank Baum, *The Lost Princess of Oz*

The great, late physicist Albert Einstein was traveling on a train one day. Shortly after the train left the station in Princeton, the conductor walked down the aisle, punching the tickets of every passenger as he went. When he came to Einstein, the brilliant but notoriously absent-minded scientist reached into his vest pocket for his ticket, but it wasn't there. He checked each of his trouser pockets. No ticket. He looked in his briefcase. No ticket. He looked on the seat beside him. No ticket.

At that point, the conductor said, "Dr. Einstein, I know who you are. We all know who you are. I'm sure you bought a ticket. Don't worry about it." Einstein nodded appreciatively. The conductor continued down the aisle punching tickets. As he was ready to move to the next car, he turned around and saw the great physicist down on his hands and knees looking under his seat for his ticket.

The conductor rushed back. "Dr. Einstein, don't worry," he said. "As I told you, I know who you are. You don't need a ticket. I'm sure you bought one."

Einstein looked at him and said, "Young man, I too, know who I am. What I don't know is where I'm going."

As this story illustrates, sometimes we need to create stories to discover where we've been or where we are going. Stories are a great way to convey information that will be remembered, so this chapter will look at knowledge/information-based stories and how they can be useful. In a nutshell, these kinds of stories are a compact, easily retained, powerful way to convey the knowledge and information that you need to communicate to your target market, whether that's employees within your company or consumers and customers out in the world.

For example, a few years ago, I was hired to work with a company to help them compile a virtual bonfire, which could be used by both old and new employees. In a nutshell, old employees could gather around the fire and tell stories both about the company history as well as the best practices and techniques used by members of the company. And then, new employees could join the bonfire and learn both about the past of the company as well as best practices and shortcuts used in the field and the office by members of the company. It was a great way to capture the culture of the company as well as to allow new employees to quickly learn about that culture.

Think about the knowledge/information stories you tell all the time. We do this constantly and hardly think about it. You walk into the copy room in a rush, push print, and then, of course, the machine gets stuck; so you go find somebody for help. An older employee walks in to help you and she tells you, "Oh my God! That always happens to me. You can't do more than 10 pages at a time and it doesn't like it when you shove the pages in too far or use the double-sided function. Once, like four years ago, it even started smoking. It almost set off the fire alarm. So I unplugged it and waved the smoke away and then waited 10 minutes and just plugged it back in and it worked great. And it helps if you talk nice to it and rub it like this." So, you unplug it and start over and—*voila!*—it works great. This kind of information/knowledge storytelling goes on all day, we just rarely think about it.

Let me give you another example. Let's look at knowledge/information stories used to deal with the issue of change in a company. Trevor Garlick, a business consultant who specializes in change management, was kind enough to offer his thoughts to me on how the right knowledge/information story can help a company survive change and I think you will find them illuminating:

RK: How do you see the role of storytelling in business today?

TG: The role of storytelling in business change is crucial. At a "big picture level," it makes the difference between creating a coherent and thorough picture that everyone can see and understand at all levels of the organization (which can be openly challenged and criticized) versus a command: "You will do this, and you will change—or you're out!"

At a more detailed level, within individual change programs and projects, for example, a system replacement or a desktop upgrade, there will be moments of enormous challenge to the team where agreement from on high is required to solve a problem. The last thing to do in this instance is throw the problem up the chain and ask for a solution. Placing the problem into context within a short though concise story can not only soften the blow, but it can relate the problem directly to the culture and the situation of the organization exactly. In other words, it can make it both understandable and palatable.

It should be remembered, at this level not only does the story have to make sense, more importantly, it has to give the executive ammunition to explain simply and in acceptable terms what is going on, how the problem came about, and why the recommended solution is the course to follow. In short, identifying and explaining the size and scale of the elephant on the table, and how to get rid of it.

Perhaps this is an over-arching narrative for the life of the change program propagated with mini-stories as required.

RK: How do you see the role of storytelling in business meetings?

TG: PowerPoint presentation can lead to the death of many business meetings, but it must be remembered that PPT is simply a format, and it can be very useful as a tool of communication when used correctly. However, it is important that narratives are used with or beyond PPT. The story that is told then must "land" properly and that it is appropriate to the audience.

For example, within the same headline "story" this will be chunked down according to the level (seniority) and size of audience, thus the format of presentation will change depending on many things, such as time constraints and the "need" for information (not the want). Also, you may want your audience to stand and physically "walk through" the story with you in a session, or you might need this to propagate around key stakeholders first to sound them out. Alternatives to this are the 30-second "elevator pitch" which serves as the hook to get your agenda onto the table. Whichever it is, to be successful, your need will be in the form of a succinct narrative.

Once you have landed a successful narrative, you should have enough credibility to be listened to in the future. The trick is to ensure you then continue to build the relationships with the important audiences to build this into a rhythm. You can then refine your storytelling with the input of feedback from your peers/seniors. This will mean each time you have the opportunity, your audience should be ready and willing to listen to you. This is important if you are on a long change journey, as you sometimes need a huge stock of "credibility chips" on your bank to successfully navigate through major business change programs.

Therefore, just as in product marketing, you need to know your audience, target the messages, build and sustain those relationships with the key stakeholders. It is simply that the messages within your stories will tend to be about internal affairs, although with key references to the customer (the usual objective behind the business change) to anchor the story into the reality of either today or the future.

RK: Can you give me some thoughts on how the stories you tell inside a company about change should and need to evolve?

TG: Within the context of a particular program, all stories need to evolve, and this will be for different reasons. For example, the holistic narrative around the whole piece of change needs to continue from concept and through and past implementation; people should be begging for your change to come down the line to them if you have done your job correctly.

Additionally, as you meet certain challenges, stories will need to be created that deal with succinct challenges or opportunities that may go to smaller segments of the overall audience, for example key stakeholders. Therefore, it is important to ensure that the narrative evolves and keeps apace with the program and its environment.

The context of today's change programs will tend to be large, complex, and rarely anything but global. This means multi-year programs are the norm, not the exception. Dealing with what might be significant change external to the change program itself—for example, major customer behavior shift that we have recently seen in UK shoppers' supermarket habits, or the effect of a merger/acquisition—both of these may call all or part of the program into question.

Being on top of this and having the capacity to get the stories out to the appropriate audiences is crucial. Ensuring that you find value for money out of the investments already made whilst being able to make the right decisions on the life or death of a program, or how to take onboard a large change of scope, can make a significant contribution in such turbulent times. Acknowledging that not everyone in a large organization will be able to do this, those who shine early will tend to get the attention of those required at the right time to ensure success continues.

RK: Can you talk about myths within a company?

TG: The death-knell of any major program is the propagation of myths that are far removed from the realities or the important truths of the situation. This can be driven by the lack of acceptance or indeed the rejection of a change program, most commonly a new piece of software, or a headcount reduction scheme by the user group(s). This is where the voice of the user is louder and more consistent with its storytelling than the program itself. Simply put, this is a story about competing stories.

One of the most challenging roles for storytelling within change programs is its use in enabling the truth, or more likely the ugly truth, to come into the open and enable the program to move forward on a secure footing. This might have to include the discrediting of various myths in circulation at the time. Not an easy task that generally requires going back to square one to understand the basic business needs of the piece of change in question.

In the very worst of cases, these stories will focus upon answering the most demanding of questions: What went wrong? How and why did this happen? Who is responsible? How much exactly did it cost, and how much more do we need to invest to get us back on track? Alternatively, how much if anything can be salvaged? Worse still, where does this figure get placed on the balance sheet?

Irrespective of the management and technical skill required to answer these questions, a story or set of stories will need to be created to get the messages out. Where this involves consequences for people's careers, care and skill are needed.

RK: What types of story are we talking about?

TG: How a headcount reduction in one country can benefit the customer when the work is to be moved to somewhere lower-cost like Eastern Europe or India. How does what is a cost-cutting exercise benefit those in the existing organization? Getting that into an understandable and acceptable story is one that is regularly required today.

This new mega-system actually makes my tasks more complicated and manual rather than automated and streamlined! This is not progress. The big picture here is important; there are winners and losers in all business change. The important thing is not to lose sight of the major objectives and to be sure of the overall business benefits.

Every executive has her/his key relationships. Each of these has a credible, trusted voice, voices that maybe change-averse, or unwilling to accept changes to their universe. The storytelling of a program needs to be able to deal effectively with this.

The inevitable "anti-stories" that appear—generally when people who are in a flux of change get nervous and voice their opinions in such a way they seek to simply discredit the program in any way possible. This needs to be understood and taken account of within the overall storytelling of the program if it is to successfully navigate through such challenges.

RK: What about emotion?

TG: The key to successful business change is a rational approach with detailed information to support the findings and activities of the program.

Anyone who doesn't support or want the change will generally respond and challenge this with powerful emotionally driven stories—perhaps wrapped in rational statistical clothing—in an attempt to discredit part of or all of a program.

Emotional debate should be left aside wherever possible. If it exists, take it off the table at the earliest opportunity. This is a cultural issue, as both countries and organizations are very different in both their basic make-up and approaches to problem-solving. However, within the context of global programs, evidence-based argument will tend to win the day.

The most common emotional heartstring is the "how will this make our people feel about (us and) the organization as a whole?" A leader with a natural disposition of "emotional" rather than "rational" will always find that question throws them into a personal flux from which they may not extricate themselves without outside help.

Emotional debate is not helpful here.

RK: How do you create the best business story/narratives you can?

TG: There is a method, though the context is always important and within a major program there is usually a stream of work, which deals with all internal (and perhaps external) communication.

This does not mean that the team will create all stories, but it will certainly be a key stakeholder in disseminating the word out of the program to large audiences.

Management of key stakeholders to the program will generally be controlled by the program director and her/his immediate team.

CHAPTER 14

Brand/Product Vision Myth

||||||||||||||||||||||||||||||||||||||||||||||||||||||||||||||||||||||||||||||||||||||||||||||||||||||||||||||||||||||||||||||||||

The most pathetic person in the world is
someone who has sight but no vision.

—Helen Keller

Sometimes, we tell stories in business to inspire and create myths or, in other instances, we develop stories to defuse or tame legends. This chapter will use the rules and tools already given in the earlier chapters to look at how stories can create heroes and bond teams together, leading to greater collaboration, greater success, and a deeper understanding of what your company represents.

Sometimes the hero of your story is one of your consumers. Look to your testimonials to get these stories. For example, take NutriBullet, "The world's first nutrition extractor." Now, whether NutriBullet really emulsifies plant matter better than your teeth can is up to you to decide, but either way, if you go to NutriBullet's Website, you can find some great stories in the testimonial section that tend to be brand/product vision myths with a bit of origin stories thrown in for good luck.

For instance, a consumer named "Etienne B." tells a story about all the ups and downs of trying to be healthy. He talks about diets he has tried and supplements he has used without being able to maintain his weight. Finally, he tells of how things got so bad that he knew he needed to make a change in his life. After a visit to the dentist and getting his teeth pulled, he had to purchase a blender because he wouldn't be able to eat solid food for a while. He visited blogs and learned about NutriBullet. He bought one and he said that it was, "Just the ticket off the roller coaster. Being able to mix green, raw vegetables with my favorite fruits and adding boosts really turned my life around. I couldn't believe how great it tasted. As if the taste wasn't good enough, I started noticing changes immediately."

He looked better, felt better, and had more energy. He made better eating choices and stopped putting junk foods in his body. He even started getting his family and friends to use NutriBullet and eat better. Today, he still uses NutriBullet and it's an important part of his life.

This is powerful stuff. We see the problem and we get a solution. It is passionate and exciting, and there is even a great before and after picture of him looking much healthier and leaner. It is good marketing and it sells a lot of NutriBullets.

Case study: financial planning

In the world of financial planning, a savvy planner must be able to tell stories that endow potential clients with a vision of the future that is comforting. This skill is crucial and, as you may have already guessed, it usually involves brand/product vision myths. Therefore, I turned to a friend, Frank Myer, a financial analyst, and he shared two stories with me about just such a situation:

Frank's story one: not knowing the characters:

I often worked with a financial advisor who would bring me in to ensure that his clients purchased the right instrument to give them financial security in the future. In this case, we met with one client, a very successful business owner in the oil and gas service industry. Let's call him Mike.

In our meeting, Mike tells us a story. When his dad passed away, the man was worth about $4 million dollars. $2 million was to go to his current wife, not Mike's mother, and then Mike and his brother were each to get $1 million.

Mike adds: "That was eight years ago. Neither my brother nor I have seen a penny of that money. What I want is something that, when I die, will pay my two daughters $2 million each."

We wrapped up the meeting a few minutes later and Mike left the office. I turned to my financial advisor (FA) friend and said, "Mike just told you he wants a $4 million life insurance policy."

FA: Well, I'm not so sure.

Me: He just told you he wants $2 million for each of his daughters. There is no better way to do this. What are their names?

FA: I didn't know he had daughters until today.

That man had no idea about the story of his client. And, you guessed it, we never ended up closing a deal or doing any business together with Mike.

Frank's story two: using a story well

I was called by another financial advisor to go with him to visit one of his clients. He had made several proposals to this client. Nothing was happening and he hadn't been able to close any deals. He was doing a little business with this client, a woman in her late 60s, but the financial advisor here wasn't seeing the movement he knew that should be happening.

I went with him and we met with "Miss B." She was very nice and you could tell she was searching for answers, but not hearing what she felt like she needed.

After hearing about the meetings where nothing happened, Miss B assured me she liked working with the financial advisor, and would continue to do so, but felt like the solutions offered weren't really for her.

Me: You like the advisor. He likes working with you. You feel like he does a good job, but something is missing. What's missing?

Miss B: I have four daughters. They keep showing me how to split my assets four ways. I don't want to do that.

Me: It's your money. You can do what you want. What's the issue that's stopping you?

Miss B: Two of my daughters work with me here. A third daughter is an ICU nurse and, unfortunately, my fourth daughter doesn't have a job and has alcohol and drug problems. If I give $3 million to her, I know it will be gone in a year.

Me: Why don't we set up a special trust fund for her that can keep that from happening?

Miss B: No. Forget it. I am not giving her a nickel.

Me: When you say, not giving her a nickel, if she got sick, would you help with medicine?

Miss B: Yes. Of course.

Me: And if your granddaughter needed a new sweater to go to kindergarten, would you pay for that?

Miss B: Yes. I would be happy to do that.

Me: What you are telling me is your daughter can't be trusted with money. You want to help, but don't want to let her have cash?

Miss B: Yes, that is what I would like.

Me: Okay, so let me tell you two stories. The first is a story about one of your daughters getting a nice chunk of cash and spending it all quickly on drugs and stuff that you'd rather her not buy. The other story has a happier ending.

It's a story about you setting up a trust fund specifically for her. In this story, you can control what money she gets and how she spends it, and you will have the peace of mind knowing that the money will be there for your granddaughter or even your daughter if she gets sick.

Result: We helped Miss B set up a trust for the fourth daughter. She was happy and felt a sense of accomplishment by doing something she knew in her heart she should do, and was protecting her daughter for the long term.

Part 4: Real-World Applications

CHAPTER 15

Using Video to Share Your Story

|||||||||||||||||||||||||||||||||||||||||||||||||||||||||||||||||||||||||||||||||||||||||||||||||||||||||||||||||||||||||||||||||||||||||||||||||||

*As bad as we are at remembering names and phone numbers
and word-for-word instructions from our colleagues, we
have really exceptional visual and spatial memories.*
—Joshua Foer, *Moonwalking With Einstein: The
Art and Science of Remembering Everything*

These days, there are myriad ways to share your stories with the world and video might be the single most powerful one. For example, there seems to be a reversal going on at Facebook: Photo posts which used to be a huge driver, are now scoring low organic reaches. Socialbakers data research shows that photo posts on Facebook brand pages now have the lowest average organic reach. The average video post is seen more than twice as often.

Further research indicates that advertising campaigns are involving video ads more and more. For example, the BrightRoll

2015 Advertising Agency Survey found that the majority of agencies believed online video advertising is as, or more, effective than TV. They also found that agencies were drastically increasing digital video budgets. In addition, they discovered that the click-through rate (the amount of times a click is made on an online ad) was declining in importance. Finally, they found that targeting capability is what's really valuable about digital video and they believe that mobile video is where the most money will be spent in the digital media realm.

So it is clear: The future belongs to video and it's incumbent upon you to use it, whether you have a big budget or a small one. All companies, no matter how tiny, must think about how they can activate consumers via video.

It's true that years ago, you would have to hire an expensive film crew to shoot anything, but these days, people are shooting nicely produced high-definition video with small cameras or even their smartphones. As with all stories, write a great script, shoot, and edit it well and you can really help the brand and increase sales.

However, with every video, there is also the chance for epic failure. Bad video can live forever online and do untold damage to your brand. So be careful here. In the end, it's up to you to focus on what you can control and that means the script, for starters.

It all starts with the script. What story are you trying to tell and how can you bring it to life on video?

Let me give you another example of how I took a small company through this whole systematic process and ended up with a great script and video. Here's the whole story:

Allison Wild is a doctor of philosophy candidate in clinical Pharmacology at the University of Oxford in England. She has a passion for responsible healthcare and, more specifically, for finding the best organic ingredients in the world for her skin- and haircare products. She is starting her own skincare line that she is calling Wild & Organic. Allison's inspiration can be traced back to her life on her grandparent's farm in Exmoor, Somerset.

In her own words:

One of my earliest memories of pain is courtesy of Urtica dioica, a common stinging nettle on Exmoor. Luckily, Nanny and Rumex obtusifolius were near at hand. My grandmother rubbed the dock leaf vigorously into my tiny toddler calf and the pain and swelling subsided. She crushed and rubbed the leaf onto my skin, as I'm sure her mother and grandmother did onto hers when she was a young girl. In other words, specific knowledge of the medical uses of plants was effectively passed down through countless generations.

Thus began my lifelong intrigue with the ethnopharmacological uses of plants. Decades later, I researched and learned that Rumex obtusifolius has anthracene derivatives and anthraquinones, such as Aloe emodin, which are found in the Aloe vera plant. There is now a proven pharmacological reason for its long-believed anti-inflammatory properties, where science comes in decades, if not centuries, later supporting what cultures that have experienced its efficacy have known to be true all along.

After completing her undergraduate degree at Brown University, magna cum laude, Allison moved to London 20 years ago. Allison founded a company in IT systems development and traveled throughout Europe designing and implementing cutting-edge systems for a variety of applications. The travel was instrumental in discovering other cultures' ethnobotanical practices and reawakened a dormant interest in effective botanical treatments. In 2005, Allison decided to devote more time to investigating botanical actives and embarked on several expeditions, also studying with professors, botanists, and dermatologists throughout Europe. Moving out of London to Oxfordshire prompted a major focus on research and development into multimolecular antimicrobials derived from concentrated plant extracts.

I asked her to give me a sense of her company and her Brand DNA. She answered, "In a nutshell, I wanted to create a scientifically advanced, cutting-edge, luxury ethical skincare. The icing on the cake is that the ingredients are organic where humanly possible, and 100 percent natural." Now, here is the rest of this interview. In it, you will see her origin story and some other brand narratives driving her products:

1. **Signature origin story:** After returning from Germany, my husband, Bruce, became very ill with rashes in various places all over his body. He would scratch whenever he could, often in his sleep, and the rashes quickly became infected, bloody wounds. His local GP prescribed antibiotics, and steroid ointments, and then diagnosed eczema.

   Neither of us had any faith in this diagnosis, however. Quickly, things got so bad that he was told that his leg was on the verge of being septic. The doctors wanted to treat it with the standard antibiotics, but Bruce used the steroid ointments. The rashes didn't heal and he still could not stop scratching, so I was constantly cleaning oozing, bleeding wounds. I even taped cotton gloves to his hands at his request, but he would rip these off in his sleep and wake up with several more bleeding sores in the morning.

   Bruce had had some adverse reactions to antibiotics in the past and we both tend to shy away from them since they have so many negative side effects, especially when the problem is topical and not yet a systemic infection.

   Then, during a site visit for work, he fell down a manhole into a sewer. The cast iron of the manhole cover scraped a large part of the skin on his shin off and injured the bone underneath. Infection rapidly set it. His doctor gave him a week's supply of amoxicillin, but no wound management advice. His leg became swollen and with every visit the doctor drew a line on his leg demarcating the extent of the systemic infection. When the line reached his groin and his toes turned black, we rushed in to the ER.

   So, here he was, on the verge of having to get his leg amputated and the medical establishment didn't seem to offer any viable answers. I knew it was up to me to do something to help heal his wounds. Time was running out and I had to respond quickly.

I set out to buy a product with both healing abilities as well as no chemicals that he could react to. After visiting several pharmacies, I was astonished, shocked, and surprised to find that there were none available. Whatsoever.

As a trained clinical pharmacologist, I had the unique ability to truly decipher and understand what's on the label of all the skincare products that are available today. With this knowledge, I was able to see what most ordinary folks can't; that most skincare products out there today are filled with tons of chemicals that don't belong on our skin.

My husband, Bruce, was now suffering badly that I had no choice but to create my own antibiotic skincare ointment that had no chemicals that Bruce's body might reject. I did so and I'm happy to say that it worked. It actually worked astonishingly well. The doctors were stunned and couldn't believe how Bruce's leg healed in two short weeks without a single prescribed, antibiotic pill or lotion from an established pharmaceutical company.

I was so moved by his recovery, and shocked by the lack of options and products available, that it changed my life. I then embarked on a series of explorations around the world (South America, Australasia, Europe, North America) looking for beneficial plants, investigating their unique and powerful qualities, which are overlooked by the industry because they are too expensive to include in products, and brought them back to England. That led me to bring one of the plants with a particularly potent molecule to the University of Oxford to do further research toward my MSc.

2. **Specific product benefits:** We offer the most scientifically advanced skincare available in the world. We make small batches, so when we make new discoveries we are able to incorporate them immediately into

innovative products. We don't have hundreds of thousands/millions of bottles sitting in our warehouse needing to be sold.

3. **Differentiator:** The key is our ability to move fast with new discoveries and get them to market.

4. Core principles, goals, and values: Support organic farmers around the world. Support fair trade projects. Never take shortcuts in offering the best to our customers no matter what the cost. Continually invest in research and development.

5. **Product or company personality:** It's all about the science. Proven evidence-based research leads to our ingredient choices. We will not compromise on ingredients and we work hard to enable their use without the need for petrochemical ingredients that other companies use to modify the feel or bulk their products out, or to make formulating easier. Even our water is expensive—distillate from steam distilling organic English lavender to make the essential oil.

6. **Company voice:** We're not cool and hip like Soap and Glory or Cowshed, we're leading edge science: technical; advanced; luxury; geeks—the science nerds of skincare.

7. **Target market:** Upscale and high end. Harrod's, Harvey Nichol's, Saks, Bendel customers. People who want results based on scientific advances and want to find a brand they can trust to deliver the results without the marketing hype, which so many distrust these days. People willing to pay for the best.

8. **Who are our competitors?** There are luxury brands that represent "hope in a jar" since they use petrochemical byproducts and huge advertising budgets, but they make their customers feel good. I don't know any scientifically advanced skincare companies. They may market as such, but it's all marketing without the ingredients to back it up.

9. **Brand identity:** I worked long and hard on this year's Aqua metallic color: non-gender specific, metallic

connoting science and cutting edge. Sans-serif fonts since they are more representative of science and modernity.

Okay, so now, how do you translate all this information into a video that can connect and engage consumers and potentially go viral? Wild & Organic is not a big company and they essentially have no budget for this. What they do have, though, is a charismatic founder who has a great story and a lot to say. True, she can't say or do it all in one short video, but I proposed to her that she try to do a series of short videos that cover several topics. Allison and anyone else, even if they are a small company, can afford to make some videos. The HD video technology on your smartphone will do if you can't afford a real film crew. Spend time on the script and make sure you get someone on camera who is comfortable talking. Shoot it. Sorry, but there are no excuses not to create video. Just take the time to make sure the script and performance are well done. If you can't get an editor, you can even shoot it in one take and, thus, have no need for one.

So, you are ready to make a video, but you are not confident on how to proceed. Well, I usually recommend doing at least one little video for each of my typologies. So that would mean one of each of the following: an origin story video, an information story video, a value story video, and a vision story.

Not knowing exactly what she wanted and what type of video would serve her best, I decided to write Allison an e-mail and ask her some questions that might lead to a good script. And boy, did I hit pay dirt!

I asked her about a bottle of skin cream that costs more than $400 because I wanted to see her take on it and how one of her products might compare. Here is the e-mail that she sent back to me:

Hiya, Prof. K! Thanks for your e-mail. Here are some thoughts for you on that incredibly expensive tiny bottle of anti-wrinkle cream and products like it.

This anti-wrinkle cream is known for its gorgeous packaging, but the ingredient choices leave a lot to be desired!

The main aim of the big expensive companies is that their products feel and smell nice, and have a good marketing story. These do for sure.

I have no doubt that even their inexpensive competitors, who are another petrochemical great, would be just as effective and no more nasty.

I wouldn't let any of this crap near my skin ever. However, their aim is not really to reduce wrinkles, but to engage a loyal following with expensive packaging and pleasant aromas. Become part of the club that uses those fine bottles. "Never mind about wrinkles! We all age and can't really do much about that!" But we can smell nice while enduring the process.

If you plastered organic olive oil or sunflower oil on your face it would be much healthier (essential fatty acids!) and infinitely more affordable.

The limit of Phenoxyethanol allowed in a product is 1 percent, so every ingredient after that, i.e., the ones that make up the marketing story, is in the product in infinitesimally small amounts.

In the end with these types of products, it's all about the marketing and nothing about the truth. Here are more details on just a few of these ingredients:

Butylene glycol (1.3-Butanediol) is a solvent and co-monomer used in polyurethane and polyester resins.

C13-16 Isoparaffin branched chain aliphatic hydrocarbons extracted from petroleum.

Dimethicone—a silicone that feels great on the skin but is occlusive. It is the main ingredient of Silly Putty!

Pentylene glycol is a synthetic, low molecular weight solvent commonly used as a plasticizer.

Ammonium Acryloyldimethyltaurate/VP Copolymer is a copolymer of ammoniumacryloyldimethyltaurate and vinylpyrrolidone monomers. YUCK! Feels nice though!

Propylene glycol is commonly used as aircraft de-icing fluid. It makes formulating easy for the lazy chemist since it forces things together.

Just briefly, here is my take on some of the ingredients for another beauty product that also costs hundreds and hundreds of dollars:

Glycerine is the cheapest humectant possible.

Alcohol seriously dries the skin and disrupts the hydrolipid layer.

Isohexadecane is a 16 carbon branched chain hydrocarbon extracted from petroleum.

Glyceryl Polymethacrylate is ester of glycerin and polymethacrylic acid. Polymethacrylic acid is a polymer made from methacrylic acid. Methacrylic acid is a carboxylic acid with an acrid unpleasant odour. Methacrylic acid is produced industrially on a large scale and has numerous uses, most notably in the manufacture of polymers such as Lucite and Plexiglas.

Butylene glycol (1.3-Butanediol) is a solvent and co-monomer used in polyurethane and polyester resins.

Propylene glycol is commonly used as aircraft de-icing fluid.

Best, Allison

ıllıllıllıllıllıllıllıllıllıllıllıllıllıllı

The question, though, still remains: How do you take all this material and create a script? Well, for starters, after reading this e-mail, I knew that we had all the ingredients necessary for a great *information* story-based script. But I had to extract the best information and transpose it into script form in order for Allison to shoot it. So here's what I did.

I tried to visualize what the audience would see and what were the most important and powerful things that Allison could say on camera. In other words, because film is a visual medium, I started thinking visually. I loved the idea of Silly Putty and de-icing fluid. I knew these would be powerful visual props that I wanted in the video. I also knew that I wanted her to be wearing a white lab coat and to shoot in her lab, where she spends every day analyzing these chemicals.

I think anyone can write scripts if they are prepared to think this way: visually. How can you convey as much information as possible without dialogue? And then, when you use dialogue, how can you say things that go beyond what we are already seeing on screen? Think in low-budget terms. Have as few actors or on-screen personalities as possible. Use as few sets as possible. A single location is best.

Also, get good sound. We all tend to focus on hair, makeup, and lighting, but forget about sound. This is a mistake. You can fix lighting issues in the post-production edit if necessary, but if the sound is bad, you are screwed. So, make sure the person who is talking has a good microphone on or near them and check sound levels constantly.

Shoot more than one angle of each moment, so you have what is called coverage. This will allow you to edit if something goes wrong with one of your shots. And shoot what is called "B Roll." This is secondary shots of things. So, in this case, I would shoot lots of footage of Allison talking and doing all the lines in the script. I would then shoot B Roll, which would entail shots of her working in the lab and not talking, as well as several shots of objects in her lab, especially the important ones, such as chemical containers and the ones relevant to this story, such as the Silly Putty and the de-icing fluid.

Here are a few final thoughts. First, in general, one page of script tends to correspond to one minute of video time, so I would recommend never going more than seven pages or seven minutes of video per script. I would also recommend writing your script in screenplay format, so I will now give you an example. Scripts tend to be pretty simplistic, so don't overwrite them. Keep the language simple and only describe what the audience would see on screen as they are watching the video. (*Int.* stands for inside and *Ext.* means outside.) Happy scripting:

||||||||||||||||||||||||||||||||||||||

Fade in:
Int. Fancy laboratory—Day
A real working chemical lab with glass beakers and things that are bubbling and alive.

Professor Wild (in white lab coat and glasses) looks up from an experiment that she is conducting and smiles.

Prof. Wild (To camera.)

"Welcome to my lab here in Oxford, England. People keep e-mailing me with questions about products they are using, so I wanted to answer a few questions about what you are really putting on your face and body."

Prof. Wild walks over to a table on the other side of the lab. As she does, she pulls an expensive skincare product out of her coat pocket in a test tube and holds it up.

Prof. Wild (To camera.)

"This product costs over $400 in the U.S. and 300 quid in England. I must admit, it's beautifully packaged and has some nice ingredients in it. But it also has some nasty ingredients—petrochemicals mostly—that I would never let touch my skin."

Prof. Wild stops at the table, which is covered in objects. She picks up a glass bottle of *olive oil*.

Prof. Wild (To camera.)

"To be honest, you'd be better off buying this organic olive oil and pouring it on your face than using that $400 jar of skin crème."

Prof. Wild puts the *olive oil* back down and picks up the expensive skin care jar.

Prof. Wild (To camera.)

"Can we get a close up of these ingredients?"

Close up—The ingredients on the label

Prof. Wild (Voice over.)

"I know some of these are really hard to pronounce, but let me tell you what these big words really mean. For example, see that word, Dimethicone—it's a silicone that feels great on the skin, but it's occlusive, which means it clogs your pores."

Pull back out—Prof. Wild lifts up a *Silly Putty* egg and opens it up. She pulls out the putty and plays with it.

Prof. Wild (To camera.)

"Dimethicone is also the main ingredient in here. And you can buy Silly Putty for only a few dollars."

Camera zooms on Prof. Wild as she picks up a *polyester* men's neck tie and then a can of *car oil* and then she puts those down and grabs a child's *plastic* toy.

Prof. Wild (Voice over.)

"Butylene glycol (1.3-Butanediol) is a solvent and co-monomer used in polyurethane and polyester resins. C13-16 Isoparaffin is branched chain aliphatic hydrocarbons extracted from petroleum. Pentylene glycol is a synthetic, low molecular weight solvent commonly used as a plasticizer."

Close shot of—Prof. Wild picks up a *vinyl* handbag and bottle of green *de-icing* fluid.

Prof. Wild (Voice over.)

"Ammonium Acryloyldimethyltaurate/VP Copolymer is a copolymer of ammoniumacryloyldimethyltaurate and vinylpyrrolidone monomers. *Yuck!* Propylene glycol is commonly used as aircraft de-icing fluid. It makes formulating easy for the lazy chemist because it forces things together."

Ext. The moors of Oxford—

Prof. Wild now wears jeans and a sweater and walks through the lush green countryside of Oxford.

Prof. Wild (Voice over.)

"So before you spend $400 on a jar of skin crème, please think about the ingredients. Your skin is too important to put petrochemicals on it, and there are too many good things out in nature that you can use that can really help."

Prof. Wild walks off into the countryside of Oxford.

Superimpose on screen—

"For more information, go to *http://wildorganicskin.com*."

Fade out.

The end.

||||||||||||||||||||||||||||||||||||

Did you see how I selected the best stuff from the e-mail to make a compelling short video? The operative word here is short. This is something you will want people to share and post and send to their friends. And they do not have the patience for a long video with too much information. The key with videos is always to be short, sweet, and to the point. Always err on the side of too short versus too long.

The other issue to always be concerned with is a potential backlash when you reveal your brand at the end of the video. If you are making a commercial, so be it. But if it seems like your video is done for socially conscious reasons and then, at the end, your brand is revealed, that revelation can undermine all that has been presented beforehand. Consumers might now see the entire video as content designed and created merely to sell product. As a result, they can feel tricked and betrayed. And an angry consumer can outright reject your message or even actively try to badmouth and hurt your brand.

So, the creation of branded content is a mighty tricky proposition. Consumers will accept sponsored videos, but if they feel like the information in the video is merely there to deceive them into buying something, your video can work against you. So, you have a choice: Either make it clear from the beginning of the video who you are and what you are up to, or at the end be subtle and don't try to sell anything.

This is the reason why I advised Allison to not mention or even put an image of her products in the video. These videos must be seen as an educational series she is doing to give people more information. And it is. Nothing is being sold at the end of the video. However, her link at the end does go to her Website, which includes both educational aspects as well as links for interested people to buy her products.

The video must play as educational and socially conscious, which it is and which is an integral part of her Brand DNA. In fact, on her Website and blog, much of her copy is purely educational and designed just to bring this kind of information to people.

And if consumers are so inspired, they can go to her Website and get more information about what is in skincare products out there today and, more specifically if they so choose, what kind of skincare products Wild Organic Bioactive Skincare is now making. Whether consumers want to use her products or not is up to them. But she will continue to be busy creating content to empower consumers with knowledge about what is in all the different skin products available out there. Then, it is up to the consumer to choose what product to purchase, based upon an informed decision.

So, it is a classic soft sell in which she is being socially responsible and doing a public service. The selling of her product is, and must be seen as, secondary, at least in this series of videos.

Scripting vs. improvisation

I am a scriptwriter by training, so I script everything. But if you are creating video content with people who are not trained actors, you might be better off doing more of what I'd call a guided improvisation, rather than a true scripted performance. I say this because if you guide the on-camera talent and prod them with questions, you might be able to get what you want from them on video without forcing your stars to follow a script and, as a result, sound, well, scripted and false.

Whether to use a script or not, in the end, is a judgment call on your part. However, look at the goal of the video and the talent involved and make an informed choice that leads to the most natural performance while still giving you the content you need. Video, unlike film, is inexpensive to shoot take after take, so do as many takes as necessary to get what you need for the editing room and the final cut. Note also that videos can be posted both on your site as well as on YouTube, on aggregate sites such as Upworthy or BuzzFeed, or other sites depending on the nature of the site and your video. Now, go out there and make some great videos that have the potential to go viral.

CHAPTER 16

Social Media and Story Sharing

||||||||||||||||||||||||||||||||||||||||||||||||||||||||||||||||||||||||||||||||||||||||||||||||||||||||||||||||||||||||||||||||||||||||||||||||||||||||||||||||

Over the past 60 years, marketing has moved from being product-centric (Marketing 1.0) to being consumer-centric (Marketing 2.0). Today, we see marketing as transforming once again in response to the new dynamics in the environment. We see companies expanding their focus from products to consumers to humankind issues. Marketing 3.0 is the stage when companies shift from consumer-centricity to human-centricity and where profitability is balanced with corporate responsibility.

—Philip Kotler

As it is so prevalent today, a discussion of storytelling cannot avoid looking at the way narratives are being constructed and altered via social media. How does the rise of social media affect your brand narrative?

This chapter will analyze the construction of brand narratives in the world of social media, their use in tribal formations and community growing, and how to best shape social media stories to lead to the greatest levels of engagement.

I think it's safe to say that with the rise of social media, the way you need to tell stories in order to achieve success has changed. By now, it should be clear that you need to do more than just list product benefits.

In our world of complete brand landscapes in which stories exist far and wide beyond the supermarket aisle, you need to show how your product or service provides an experience that adds value to someone's life through fulfilling a need or satisfying a desire. You need to connect with your customers via a strong brand narrative that translates into all forms of digital media, as well as social media.

In order to ensure consistency in how your brand is perceived, every touch point that a consumer has with you and your product must revolve around your Brand DNA and the narrative that emerges from it. This is something you can control, but it all starts with your brand narrative and how you translate that into video and language-based content that is delivered via the Internet.

In the past, you would create a brochure or a print ad or TV commercial with information that you wanted to convey to consumers. If it was a new product, you would list your primary attributes to create awareness. If it was an older known product in which listing the primary attributes felt redundant and unnecessary, you would talk about how it is new and improved and list the new and improved attributes. Or, if there happened to be nothing new and improved about your product or service, you would talk about some other qualities not previously mentioned. For example, Pepsi now no longer needs to discuss what a cola is or what Coke tastes like, so they have moved on to defining emotional properties that they want to associate with Pepsi, such as positive uplifting experiences that are associated with their new "Out of the Blue" campaign.

What you might have noticed with all of the above is that none of it is narrative based. As I have already pointed out, traditional brand communication tends to generally employ non-narrative methods to sell and, in many cases today, these methods now seem rather outmoded. To convey your message today, many times you have no choice but to employ a brand narrative because it is one of the few methods left to create engagement and interest among a cynical consumer who has seen it all.

These traditional non-narrative selling methods might at first help to further you brand, but they are essentially a one-way street in which you can focus on a few main points you want to convey. Then, you put that message out to consumers and hope that they get it. Period. Pray and see. So, it is a game of chance and prayers wherein you usually create little engagement and have little means to gauge success.

Today, the game and the rules have changed. The age of the one-way non-narrative street is over. Brand narratives are now the basis of a conversation in which you have a chance to frame the narrative and set the tone for the conversation where your stories and then consumer's narratives are shared by all: brand creators, marketers, users, and customers. If you don't frame it well, your story and your brand can run away from you and the conversation can be dictated by your consumers for good or, potentially, for bad. Consumers are empowered in a way they have never been before, and if you can't set the stage with your brand narrative, there is a good chance that the story can turn on you and potentially provide great harm to your brand.

If you understand the need for story and why your particular narrative conveys the Brand DNA of your company, that story can become the touchstone for all conversations about your company or product. You can control the online conversation instead of being controlled by it.

So rewrite and activate your brand by learning about the story you are telling and how you can improve that story, so that it will both frame the conversation about your product and company as well as inspire consumer stories that build off your narrative.

Set the tone for online and offline brand narratives that will lead to the future success of your company and product.

The question then becomes *how*? How does one gain control and become empowered in an age when the consumer seems to have all the muscle? Well, let's start with the language of your story. If knowledge and language are power, you need to really consider the content and language of your brand narratives and then compare that to the information and language captured in the many forms of social media.

What this means is that you need to look at the concerns that are raised by your consumers and tell stories that extinguish these concerns. You need to look at the very language that your customers are using and embrace that language.

What terms are coming up often? If you reflect the language that you see your customers using online, they will be more open to receiving your message. Speak in their words, but at the same time, craft their words to fit into your new brand narrative.

In his wonderful blog on copywriting, the talented and gifted copywriter, Joel Klettke gives some specific places that you can mine to find the language you need for your new business narratives:

- Reviews—These are what your customers will be looking at, too—so finding objections in reviews gives you a chance to write copy that addresses them or cuts people off at the pass before they even worry about it.
- Testimonials—These help you understand who your customers are and how they talk about your solution. You can get some real gems from here!
- Forums—The most raw, unbiased conversations on the Web, these are great for recon on your benefits and shortcomings—as well as those of your competitor.
- Q&A Sites—From Quora and Yahoo Answers right down to the lesser-known hubs, these help you understand what questions or pain points people are dealing with.
- Your Sales Team—Nobody knows your customer better. Your sales people will know the questions they're constantly being asked and the objections

your customers have, as well as the things they share that are able to push customers toward making the purchase.

- Your E-mails—Hardly anyone uses these, but don't overlook 'em! These are conversations you can mine for important intel."

So be brave and release your highly tuned, finely crafted brand narratives to the social media world. And then sit back and get ready for the onslaught. The world of social media will give you tons of feedback, whether you want it or not. So, take all that great raw material and mine it for all its worth. Be part of the conversation, connect, and stay connected.

CHAPTER 17

Yeah, But if You Don't Tell it Right

||||||||||||||||||||||||||||||||||||||||||||||||||||||||||||||||||||||||||||||||||||||||||||||||||||||||||||||||||||||||||||||||||||||||||||

It's not what you say, it's what people hear.
—Frank Luntz, *Words That Work*

No matter how well-written and well-constructed your story is, if you are doing a talk and you don't present it well, your story will inevitably fail you. As Frank Luntz says, "It's not what you say, it's what people hear" and so, then, it becomes incumbent upon you to make them hear the right thing. You've worked so hard on your story that you don't want to let it and your brand down. So now, you have to work on the presentation of that story. How do you tell it well so they hear what you want them to hear?

To answer this question, let's look at the act of telling a story. Many people tell me that they are not comfortable in front of an audience and this is one of their biggest fears. In this chapter, therefore, we will cover some basic fundamental presentational skills that will help anyone, no matter how comfortable or experienced you are in front of a crowd.

Let's take this step by step. You've done the hard work of constructing a well-structured story. You want to use it at the beginning of your speech to frame your presentation. So what's next? What are the basic things to keep in mind? How do you do it so that you appear relaxed and really deliver the goods?

Through the years, I've worked with businesspeople, executives, and lawyers on presentations for big and small events. Many times, I've brought in Hollywood acting coach, writer, and actress Jayne Amelia Larson. When we work together, I focus on the text of the material to be presented and she focuses on the physical aspects of the presentation. Jayne Amelia is a master of helping transform people's presentation and presentational skills. So, I was thrilled to ask her a whole host of questions that I thought might be of use to anyone who has to tell a story.

I feel fortunate that Jayne Amelia agreed to share some of her knowledge with me here. Let's go deeper now and explore the act of storytelling by having her give us some answers to the key questions I raised.

RK: How do you stand?

JL: Isn't it strange that as soon as we have to speak in front of an audience, many of the simplest and most common activities become onerous or awkward? So how do you stand when you've forgotten how? Or suddenly become incapacitated by sweaty palms, incontrollable shaking, and wobbly knees?

First of all *breathe*...then breathe again...then again.

Know that the most important thing is to make yourself comfortable—this will always enable you to tell a better story. If you're working from a secure and grounded place, you will more easily access your preparation, intellect, and imagination, and relaxed even breathing will help you do that. Then you're home free.

The Mountain Pose (Tadasana) practiced in yoga is a good place to start and a stance that we all do naturally in some variation or another: Stand upright with legs about hip width apart; legs straight but not locked; knees soft but not bent. Roll gently back and forth and side to side, then settle when you feel your weight evenly distributed on your feet. Focus your eyes on the near horizon, making sure to dip the chin rather than tilt it up. Lift your sternum and, at the same time, widen your shoulders and upper back muscles so that they softly release back; arms should hang loosely by your sides. Once this is achieved, you may want to experiment placing one foot slightly in front of the other and adding some turnout for more comfort.

Many people are unsure what to do with their hands; keep them loose and open by your sides unless using them to gesture. Refrain from shoving them in pockets, clasping them tightly together in front of you, or balling them into fists when nerves kick up. Practice letting them be loose so that you can use them more effectively. If you have trouble doing this, practice speaking while holding a heavy book in each hand to prevent yourself from using your hands in habitual but non-demonstrative ways.

Feel free to move about when you are speaking, and don't get stuck in any one place unless you are confined for technical reasons. Avoid using a podium to hide behind unless you absolutely have to (because the full body tells a better story than the torso alone), but also be careful not to wander aimlessly or pace back and forth frenetically when you are speaking. This is off-putting to an audience. Move as you do in real life. Stand still if needed in order to better convey a point, back up to give your audience some space to consider what you've just said, move toward them to emphasize an idea, switch direction to indicate a change in thought, etc. Try to be still as much as you can unless you have a reason to move (or ideally to gesture as detailed below).

Remember that your audience is likely watching you very intently, and that every little movement conveys a message whether you mean it to do so or not. Your audience picks up conscious and unconscious messages on many channels simultaneously, there's constant chatter, and you want to control as much of that communication as you can. If you fiddle with coins in your pocket, toy with your hair, or click your pen over and over, you are undermining your message by highlighting your discomfort. If your eyes dart to the door every time you hear it open, your audience will want to focus there too. Keeping your eyes glued to the ground as you speak, instead of trying to connect with your audience with an easy and attentive eye gaze, makes you seem afraid, disinterested, or overly self-absorbed, depending on what else is going on at the same time. Make eye contact often even when reading from a script; it's nice for everyone.

Be aware of your conscious choices when presenting, and know that your conscious choices don't have to be inauthentic ones. You can make regular conscious use of verbal and non-verbal communication, including posture, vocal tone and pitch, eye contact, facial expression, and physical gesture to help make your story dynamic and engaging. Find what works and feels right for you. You'll know immediately when that's true.

RK: How should you try to speak? In other words, how should you use your voice?

JL: Your body and your voice are powerful tools to enhance communication, and also easily trainable. They can be conditioned just like a muscle to support your storytelling. Many people have difficulty speaking fluently and with ease when they are nervous or unaccustomed to public speaking. As with all of my techniques, you must rehearse regularly out loud and often; the more you do, the easier it will get, and the better you will perform. Practice alone or on your family and friends, not in front of a mirror.

It's important that you find your own best voice with a natural sound that has the most vigorous resonance possible, and use that at all times, as much as you can in real life as well as presentation. This means utilizing as many of your resonators as possible: the bones in your face, nasal cavity, mouth, chest, etc. For each of us, the balance is different and this makes our voices unique. Nasal resonance is important to add brightness and clarity for better projection; chest resonance adds deeper tones to create warmth. Too much nasal resonance is grating on the ear, while too much chest resonance sinks and muffles the voice. Play around when speaking to discover new tones and undertones to your voice, and try to incorporate them to make a fuller sound. Finding your own best voice is a fine-tuning process of nurturing what comes most naturally to you while developing nuance, strength, and flexibility. This is most often done with a trained vocal coach, but can be achieved at home with pointed exercises from vocal technique sources that you can easily find online.

Generally, most of us need to slow down when speaking in front of an audience. You still want to be conversational, but slow down. This is particularly true at the beginning of a talk (in front of a handful of people or a thousand) when the audience's ears need to adjust to the timbre and tone of your voice to understand you better. On very important points, put a little air between the phrases; this is a way to alert your audience to pay closer attention to what you're saying. Don't run on and on like a runaway train without ever taking a breath. Use pauses occasionally to give your audience a rest as they digest an idea. Be mindful that you don't collapse vocally in tone or volume at the end of sentences, or fall into a regular mind-numbing cadence; both quickly put an audience to sleep.

RK: What do you do in terms of your gestures and at what moments in the story should you use a gesture?

JL: Gesture is your most variable and valuable tool when conveying a story. Gestures are movements made with a part
of the body in order to express meaning or emotion, or
to communicate an instruction, and can also demonstrate
an action intended to communicate feelings or intentions.
They can and should be very specific. The combination of
posture and gestures is called phrasing, and the great com-
municators are those people who match their phrasing
with their communicative intentions. Watch one of your
favorite presenters and you'll see that this is true. (TED
Talks at *www.ted.com/talks* is a great source.)

One of the very first things I teach in my workshops
is how to develop a repertoire of useful, universal, and
readily identifiable gestures to better communicate a story.
Extending your arm out in front of you, palm facing out,
immediately suggests *stop*. You can use this to reinforce a
multitude of messages: stop what you're doing, I stop myself
(us, you), stop—it's finished, etc. Moving your hands out
in front slightly away from your body with palms up, and
curling the fingers toward you suggests *come*. You can
use this literally as in *come* here, and also figuratively as
in *come*, you understand me, yes? Track the gestures you
do throughout the day and you will see that you are constantly using gesture to communicate better. You squint
your eyes and frown (gestures can be made with the face
alone) to indicate suspicion, doubt, or derision. You raise
your eyebrows in surprise (you might also gasp because
gesture can be reinforced with the voice). You clasp your
hands together to beg, etc.

Go through your text and experiment with gestures
that help you tell your story better by illustrating your
ideas, messages, and intentions. A good example I use in
my coaching is this: I ask my audience to imagine a rainbow with a pot of gold at the end. Simply saying the words
is not nearly as effective as saying them while I gesture.
Tracing the arc of a rainbow in the air high in front of me

with my hand, followed by punching then opening it so that the fingers splay at the end of the phrase, then cupping my hands as if catching something precious, immediately conjures up a vibrant mental image of a rainbow with a pot of gold at its end teeming with coins. Using my voice to depict the rainbow's arc (from low to high) and vocalizing the happy surprise of discovery of the pot of gold at the end of the arc deepens the mental image. We "see" the image in our minds, it activates the imagination, and the mind's eye is a forceful communication device. If you can find several illustrative gestures to support key points in your story, you will automatically be telling it better.

RK: What words do you emphasize and why?

JL: You should mark your speech so that you know the most important points and the specific words or phrases to highlight those points with vocal variation and gesture. Don't choose too many words in one phrase, or too many phrases on one section. Be selective and judicious, or your audience will be overwhelmed and won't be able to focus their mind energy. If you emphasize every other word, your speech becomes overly emphatic and pedantic. If you don't use emphasis at all, your speech becomes droning. Practice speaking without constant disfluencies (ums, ahs), which are usually unintentional and contribute little to the storytelling.

RK: How can you use dialogue and accents to improve the story?

JL: Good storytelling means using descriptive language and dynamic energy that fosters emotional connection and understanding. If you are good at accents or duplicating dialogue to create dramatic tension or conflict, by all means do so; it can only improve your storytelling. If you don't have those innate gifts, don't be concerned. You can still use your expressive body and voice in many ways to convey meaning and make impact. Be careful of using dialogue unless you can clearly convey who is speaking at all times. Dialogue that is poorly defined muddies any story.

But good dialogue told well helps move a story along in a conversational and real way.

RK: Where do you want to get laughs?

JL: Anywhere you can. And I mean that. Do whatever you can to make your audience laugh even if, especially if, it means embarrassing yourself. It will be winning. Comic relief is terrific for the storyteller and the audience. It feels good and it helps everybody relax. Many people suggest working on a prepared joke to deliver at the beginning of a speech to help loosen up the crowd; and if you have one in your back pocket that kills, by all means use it. Often, I have found that exercising a subtler (and more organic) form of humor is more effective and also easier for many people. Be real and in the moment, and respond. It's that simple. If you're naturally self-deprecating, use it and make a joke about yourself. If you're nervous, use it. If you're flying high, use it. If you're unprepared or over-prepared, use it. If you sprayed water all over yourself in the restroom moments before, use it. Use anything and everything at your disposal.

You can get up in front of an audience, stare at them in silence for a moment, then say, "Wow, what a good-looking crowd! How did I get in here?" and get a laugh—if you mean it. By the way, you can also tell a truly compelling story with no punch lines. You don't need humor to win your audience. Just be authentic and they will want to listen. Show them who you are. Allowing yourself to be vulnerable is a source of strength; while the fear of feeling embarrassed or ashamed is debilitating to the imagination and the intellect, and inhibits the storyteller in terrible ways. I encourage you to just let go and be yourself, with all your foibles and all, and you will be happier and freer when presenting. If you are authentic in your communication, you will be more trustworthy and therefore more credible and compelling.

RK: How do you overcome stage fright?

JL: We all experience this to some degree, even the most experienced performers, and it's natural, even healthy really. It means you're alive. If you didn't have nerves, you wouldn't be conscious. The best thing you can do is to embrace the stimulus and use the energy to pump yourself up in a positive way. Adrenalin is a fantastic catalyst and is probably the backbone of all great achievement.

If you are so terrifically nervous or agitated before you present that you can barely see or hear (and that happens), use your breath to settle yourself. Focus on listening to the regular inhalation and exhalation of your automatic energetic body by cupping your palms around your ears; this will calm you within moments. Severe sufferers of stage fright should try the Sarnoff Squeeze, developed by the actress Dorothy Sarnoff, whose purpose is to block the body's production of noradrenaline or epinephrine, the body's fear-producing chemicals. If you are interested in this technique, you can find out more about it online. But essentially, it entails sitting straight up in a chair, leaning forward slightly, putting your hands together in front of you, and pressing them together as you exhale and then inhale repeatedly and forcefully. You can also practice this pressing against a wall as well. If you do this right, you can feel the squeeze do its work and it does really relax you.

But the real trick to help you deal with stage fright is increasing your comfort level by rehearsing—regularly practicing in front of an audience—so that you can learn what to expect from your energetic system when you are nervous, excited, or confused. When you discover you get a dry mouth making it difficult to speak, you learn to have water nearby; if you know you sweat profusely, you learn to have a handkerchief handy to subtly wipe your face; if you notice that your eyes have trouble focusing to easily read your text, you learn to use 16-point type when printing it out (this is an excellent trick!), etc. All of these adjustments can be made easily, but only if you have prior knowledge that they may be needed because they've been experienced and noted in rehearsal or practice.

RK: What specific acting techniques can be applied to presentations that might help anyone?

JL: Rehearse. Rehearse. Rehearse. And do it again. I promise you that is your golden ticket. Repetition and rehearsal help to develop neural pathways that aid in the learning and execution of technique. The author and educator Tony Buzan says that "...repetition itself increases the probability of repetition. The more times a 'mental event' happens, the more likely it is to happen again." I have observed this to be true many times in my coaching. Also, know your material and you will tell it better. Connect with your material by using your mind and body to convey it, and exercise your imagination to emotionally translate what you are saying in an authentic and meaningful way. Don't force it. Just be real. The bottom line is that your authenticity will sell your story every time. Once you start to try to behave like somebody else, to attempt to sound like your boss, or to act like someone different, it will all fall apart. Your audience senses disingenuousness.

RK: What is your goal in terms of creating emotions during your story and how do you do that?

JL: I know you already talked about mirror neurons in this book, but I will reference them again here. Mirror neurons are the source of our empathetic understanding, and it should be your paramount goal as a presenter to connect with your audience by using this phenomenon of communication. Recent science has proven that this effect (which basically can be broken down to Monkey See/Monkey Do) is a powerful link to empathy and better communication. Using voice and gesture to create mental images that conjure up emotion acts as an organic conduit to reflexive understanding. Your audience empathizes more with you the better they understand you. Descriptive text deepens the connection and makes messages more meaningful, more "sticky," and more compelling. Emotional empathy is the foundation of all good storytelling even if, and perhaps especially if, your audience has little practical knowledge of the world of your story. The emotional connection that you create for them with your body and your voice helps them to understand something they've never actually experienced or witnessed, and yet they begin to know it because they feel it through you, the storyteller. It's a wonderful thing.

CHAPTER 18

The Magic of Story

*There is no greater agony than bearing
an untold story inside you.*
—Maya Angelou, *I Know Why the Caged Bird Sings*

To conclude, I'd like to share with you some final thoughts on the power of narratives.

Heart-centered

As you continue to think about the ideas in this book and hone your storytelling skills with all the tools presented in these pages, I hope your index finger that may once have been pointing up at your head is now pointing down toward your heart.

And, if you allow yourself to be more heart-centered, I believe you will also find that your stories are more effective and more resonant with the hearts and minds of your customers and consumers.

With power comes responsibility

Now, before this book ends, here's a caveat. In 1950, a great story-teller, William Faulkner, upon accepting the Nobel Prize for Literature said: "The poet's, the writer's, duty is...to help man endure by lifting his heart, by reminding him of the courage and honor and hope and pride and compassion and pity and sacrifice which have been the glory of his past. The poet's voice need not merely be the record of man, it can be one of the props, the pillars to help him endure and prevail" (*The Faulkner Reader*).

Faulkner knew that stories have tremendous potential power and, also, that tremendous responsibility comes with that power. In response to Faulkner's call to arms, I hope this book has inspired you to try to harness that power and has ennobled and inspired you to gladly bear that awesome responsibility.

True, storytelling is an art form that you will not be able to master overnight. But becoming a great storyteller is a truly wor-thy goal, and I wish you well on your journey toward true story mastery.

A little bit o' magic

I hope you have found many of my hints on constructing compel-ling narratives helpful. Ideally, by the time you've gotten to this final chapter, you are already on your way to creating some new killer brand narratives.

I also hope that I haven't ruined watching TV or movies for you, because now you are probably over-analyzing and deconstructing the narratives you watch. But rest assured, the best storytellers are so good that, no matter how overly analytical and well-educated you are on the craft of narrative construction, truly great stories will sweep you off your feet, and you will be so carried away that you won't notice a thing until the story is over.

In the end, though, after all the rules and guidelines and check-lists, there really is only one guaranteed way for you to become a better storyteller: keep reading great stories, keep trying to construct them, and keep practicing telling your own stories, always noting your audience's response and constantly revising, revising, revising.

Never forget, when storytelling is done well, it's truly magical. Sure, I can lecture on this stuff until I'm blue in the face (and I have). But once in a while, when you work hard at it and intuitively absorb all the rules, a great story may just burst forth from your heart. What you may find is that, if your story has just the right combination of characters, themes, and dialogue, it fuses together to enchant hearts everywhere it goes.

When told well, your story will gain a life of its own. It may even grow wings and take flight.

I want to end this book with a nod to that which is beyond our control: the magical aspects of storytelling. For, by now, you should realize that when you put the right words together and in the right order, magic really can happen.

I'm talking about the magic of a combination of sentences flying through the ether and emotionally affecting strangers, making them laugh or cry or maybe even changing the way they see the world.

I'm referring to the everyday magic of people being moved by stories. This, my friend, is not some fantastic, fictional Harry Potter–like dream. Magic happens every day when a good story is well told, and it has been happening for centuries and millennia.

Such is the alchemy of transformational narratives, the enchantment of a good yarn that sheds light into the dark corners of our world. In the end, isn't that why we tell tales? To change things, to help others, to inspire growth, to teach, and to learn.

Yes, if you're good at it, and also a little bit lucky, maybe once in a while your stories will improve the lives of others on this spinning blue planet.

So that is all.

Be bold. Be brave. Hook 'em by telling better stories, embrace the magic, and keep trying to change the world for the better.

INDEX

ABOUT THE AUTHOR

Richard W. Krevolin ("Prof. K.") is a consultant, playwright, screenwriter, and professor who leads workshops around the world on all aspects of storytelling. A graduate of Yale University, Richard went on to earn a master's degree in screenwriting at UCLA's School of Cinema-Television, and a master's degree in playwriting and fiction from USC.

For many years, he was an adjunct professor of screenwriting at USC School of Cinema/TV. Under his guidance, his students have sold film scripts and TV shows to Universal, Sony-Tri-Star, Warner Brothers, Paramount, DreamWorks, and numerous other studios and production companies. He has also been a professor at Ithaca, Univ. of Georgia, Emerson, UCLA, and Pepperdine.

He wrote, produced, and directed the full-length documentary film, *Making Light in Terezin*. He is the author of multiple books, including *Screenwriting from the Soul* (St. Martin's Press), *Pilot Your Life* (Prentice-Hall), *How to Adapt Anything Into a Screenplay* (Wiley & Sons), and *Screenwriting in the Land of Oz* (Adams Media/Writer's Digest Books).

Professor Krevolin works with agencies and companies on storytelling to develop a new brand identity and to improve the power and impact of all communications, whether internal or external, including in-person, TV, radio, the Internet, and print.

During the past two decades, Professor Krevolin has flown around the world to teach the art of communication and storytelling to executives, creatives, and brand managers at many different companies, including Vaseline, Google, Pepperidge Farms, J. Walter Thompson, Ogilvy, Mullen, Panera Bread, Tata Interactive Software, Pond's Skin Care, Sunsilk Shampoo, Lux Soap, Lifebuoy, and Nike.

He has also worked with various top-tier corporate in-house and outside counsels on strategic communication and trial themes for major litigation cases.

Krevolin is the author of several young adult novels and more than 20 stage plays, and he has several scripts in development in Hollywood, including *SAFER* with Tom DeSanto Productions (*X-Men*; *Transformers*). He is one of the writers of the documentary film, *Fiddler on the Roof: 30 Years of Tradition*.

Krevolin's stage play *Trotsky's Garden*, was a finalist for the Eugene O'Neill National Playwrights' Conference. His one-man show *Yahrzeit*, a finalist in the HBO New Writer's Project, was a huge hit at the Santa Monica Playhouse, running for five sold-out months. Under a new name, *Boychik*, it opened Off-Broadway at Theater Four in New York City. Krevolin also received a Valley Theatre League nomination for best director and best play for his one-man musical *RebbeSoul-O*. His Off-Broadway stage play, *LANSKY* was recently nominated for an Outer Critics Circle Award and was a big hit at the National Yiddish Theater in Tel Aviv. His play *King Levine* opened at the Odyssey Theater in Los Angeles under the direction of Joseph Bologna and, after receiving rave reviews, it transferred to The Tiffany. It was also nominated for an Ovation Award as Best Adaptation. His plays have been performed with Renee Taylor, Joseph Bologna, Ed Asner, Allen Arbus, David Proval, Jean Smart, Mackenzie Phillips, and Richard Kline.

Krevolin has been a panelist and keynote speaker at a variety of international writers' conferences, including the Maui Writers Conference, the Santa Fe Screenwriters Conference, the Hollywood Film Festival, the Surrey Writer's Conference, the Kenyan

Screenwriters Seminar in Nairobi, and the Hollywood Film School in Kiev, Ukraine.

His consulting work has affected hundreds of TV commercials produced all over the world, many of which have won awards, including a Golden Lion at Cannes and The People's Choice Award in China. Krevolin continues to consult with marketing executives, CEOs, lawyers, writers, and brand executives privately. He also lectures and leads creative workshops worldwide.

To reach Professor K., e-mail RKrevolin@yahoo.com or visit *ProfK.com* and *PowerStoryConsulting.com*.